SPAFFORD'S
❧ 1824 ❧
GUIDE FOR
NEW YORK
TRAVELLERS

Horatio Gates Spafford
a Pocket Guide for the Tourist and
Traveler, along the line of the Canals,
and the interior commerce of the state
of New York
(T. and J. Swords, New York 1824)

Including maps of
Hudson River, Erie and Champlain Canals

Compiled by
G. MARTIN SLEEMAN

ISBN 0-932052-62-2

H.G. Spafford's *a Pocket
Guide for the Tourist and Traveler* was
reproduced from an original copy
provided by the

NEW YORK STATE LIBRARY
Albany, N.Y.

Book design by
John D. Mahaffy

Printed by Boonville Graphics, Boonville, New York

Horatio Gates Spafford
(1778-1832)

With the opening of the Erie and Champlain canals and the use of steam boats, the 1820's saw a great increase in travel in New York State creating a need for a guide for travelers and businessmen. Horatio Gates Spafford, who had just completed a 690-page 1824 edition of *Gazetteer of the State of New York*, was in an excellent position to provide such an item.

The "lucky star" was not shining over Tinmouth, Vermont on the 18th of February, 1778. Except for the date and place of Spafford's birth little is known of his early years other than he attended school in Virginia and may have taught afterwards. He came to New York State in 1800 and married Hannah Bristol. Around that time he became a member of the Society of Friends.

While his father, John, had fought to achieve freedom, Horatio devoted his life to its promotion and preservation. He believed that this could best be accomplished by universal education provided by a common school system. In 1809, convinced that the geography of the United States was not being properly presented in the school, he published *General Geography*, a work that had required eight years to prepare. He did not limit the book to geography. It contains about half as many pages of natural philosophy as it does geography. There are chapters covering: the earth, solar system, maps and globes, different languages, systems of religion and government, the development of the calendar, and extensive geographical tables. The last chapter ranges from decimal arithmetic to the improvements and discoveries from Creation to the present time. As the book was so broad in scope it did not receive general acceptance.

In 1813 he published the first gazetteer for New York State. It had taken Spafford three years to do the research and the expenditure of $7,000, $2,000 of which he had received as a loan from the state legislature. To get the gazetteer printed, Spafford assigned the copyright to his printer, who went bankrupt, leaving him with the responsibility of repaying the loan.

In June 1815, Spafford began publishing *American Magazine - a monthly miscellany*. As the publisher was a friend of, and corresponded with, several political leaders and scholars, many of them contributed ariticles for his magazine. Several of the articles he wrote himself using the pseudonyms of Americans, Franklin, and Agricola. Due to financial problems and poor health, the twelfth, and final edition, was not published until February 1817. In an attempt to recoup his losses he wrote a novel, *The Mother-In-Law or Memoirs of Madam de Morrville*. Not wanting to be known as the author, he had it published in Boston using the name Maria-Ann Burlingham.

Spafford wrote this 190-page book in just twenty days.

In 1817, under the name of "Agricola" he published a pamphlet entitled *Hints to Emigrants, on the Choice of Lands* advising newcomers on the best land to purchase and how to become successful farmers. With the failure of the *American Magazine* Spafford decided to put his knowledge to practical use. He purchased 10,000 acres in Venango county, Pennsylvania, at a dollar an acre. He moved there establishing Spafford's Settlement, imported winter wheat from Africa, and attempted to develop his holdings. As with Spafford's other endeavors this one also failed as his title to the land was challenged. Broken in health and wealth, though not in spirit, in 1820 he moved to Ballston Spa, New York, where for a short time, he published *The Saratoga Farmer*.

He began gathering material for a new edition of the gazetteer which was not to be a rehash of his 1813 edition. It took Spafford, working ten to twelve hours, six days a week, two and a half years to complete. He had sent out over 1,100 letters, 800 written in long hand, to every postmaster and town official in the state. He also traveled extensively and hired men to visit those areas where he had not received sufficient information. From the extensive information he had gathered for the gazetteer he was able to compile *A Pocket Guide for Tourist and Traveler*.

A second edition was issued in 1825. That year

also saw his last published work, *The New York Pocket Book* (William S. Parker, Troy, N.Y.).

As was common during the time, Spafford was a gentleman-scientist. He was especially interested in the physics of heat, metallurgy and mechanics. In 1805 he was granted a patent for an "Improved Fireplace" which he favored over stoves. The latter, he believed, were "injurious to the majority of constitutions." That year he also published a pamphlet on the chemical properties of iron. On 25 March, 1814 he patented a "wheel carriage" using a U-shaped axle. The inventor claimed that the design would reduce the power required to pull the carriage by one quarter. However, it required using seven-foot wheels. Spafford also proposed using a bladder filled with air instead of springs.

Until 1856, when Bessemer invented a process for making steel in quantity, steel could only be produced in a limited amount and by a time consuming method. Spafford, on 30 October 1822, was granted two patents for the production of steel that was essentially the method developed by Bessemer three decades later. Spafford offered this patent to the United States Government provided that he receive one third of its worth and the production was marked as "Spafford Iron" or "Spafford Cast Steel." The method was also offered to the Emperor of Russia, but we do not know on what terms. The lack of acceptance of Spafford's invention was largely due to his failure to fully describe the process. He was by nature secretive, and also at that time, a patent gave the inventor very little protection. Once a new idea was published it could, and usually was, used by others without the payment of royalties. Spafford campaigned, with some success, to have the patent law 'changed. On 19 December 1822 he was granted a patent for "Tool Edges." At the present time we do not know the nature of this invention. His 1822 patents were lost when the patent office was destroyed by fire on 15 December 1836.

In 1827 Spafford wrote to Professor Amos Eaton, of the newly founded Rensselaer Polytechnic Institute, that he had invented an engine that would operate a boat, carrying a load of 15 tons, at a speed of 20 miles per hour. In essence his proposed engine would use a water wheel submerged in a container of water (see exhibit A). Compressed air, by means of an air pump, fig. 1, A, would enter at the bottom of the container so that air bubbles would raise the buckets in contrast to the normal water wheel where the weight of the water, and gravity, operates the wheel. He also planned to pass the air on to other units, fig. 1, B, another attempt to achieve perpetual motion. His compressed air motor might have worked, but probably would not have achieved the power the inventor claimed. It is doubtful Spafford's idea of using steam, fig. 2, would have been successful.

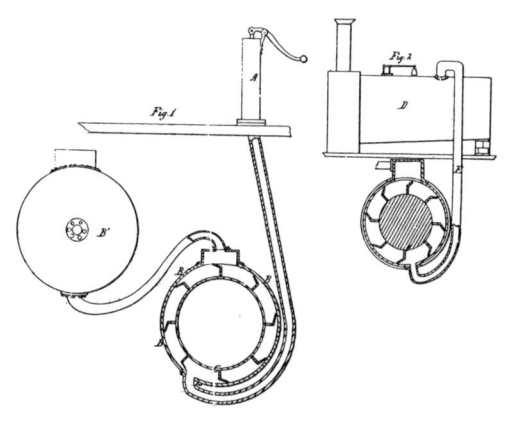

Exhibit A, Spafford's
Compressed Air & Steam Engines

Spafford died before he was granted a patent for his engine so it was issued to his second wife, Elizabeth (Clark Hewitt), on 3 July 1833. Spafford had, on 4 October 1832, added a codicil to his will appointing Canvas White as his executor as he "understands the principle of my discovery and will, in the event of my death, be able to act usefully for my heirs and estate." Canvas White (1790-1834) had invented a process for making hydraulic cement using locally available material. This made the construction of locks for the Erie Canal economically feasible; he also served as the canal's principle engineer. Even after death fate was not kind to Spafford. Mr. White might have developed the compressed air engine but, due to illness, he moved to Florida and survived the inventor by less than two years.

If Spafford's method of processing iron ore had been pursued it is likely the benefits of steel would have been available several decades earlier. One of the requirements for success is "being in the right place at the right time." Horatio Gates Spafford was ahead, way ahead, of his time.

Steamboat *Clermont*,
watercolor by Richard Varick DeWitt
Courtesy of the New York Historical Society, New York City

Packet Boat at Lock at Rome,
N.Y. miniature painting by Ben Dale
Courtesy of the Rome Historical Society

Rochester-Canandaigua Stage

Stagecoach
Richard F. Palmer, The Old Line Mail,
North Country Books, Utica, N.Y.

BIBLIOGRAPHY

Boyd, Julian P., *Horatio Gates Spafford, Inventor, Author, Promoter of Democracy*, (Worchester, Mass: Proc. Amer. Antiquarian Society, 1942, Vol. 51) pp. 279-350.

_____, *Horatio Gates Spafford, Precursor of Bessemer*, (Proc. Amer. Philosophical Society, Vol. 87, No. 1, July 1943) pp. 47-50.

Early Unnumbered United States Patents (1790-1836) Woodbridge, CT: Research Publications Inc. 1980)

A

POCKET GUIDE

FOR

THE TOURIST AND TRAVELLER,

ALONG THE LINE OF THE

CANALS,

AND THE

INTERIOR COMMERCE

OF THE

STATE OF NEW-YORK.

———

BY

HORATIO GATES SPAFFORD, LL. D.

AUTHOR OF THE GAZETTEER OF NEW-YORK.

———

NEW-YORK:

PRINTED BY T. AND J. SWORDS,

No. 99 Pearl-street.

1824.

Price 50 Cents.

PREFACE.

A SMALL Directory for the Pocket, embracing the vast extent of the lines of natural and artificial navigation in this State, has become no less a desideratum with tourists and travellers than with men of business,—the merchant, farmer, transporter, boatman, and all descriptions of persons, whose interest or curiosity is excited by the new and novel course of business and events among us. To supply this want, is the object of this small volume. That it might embrace as great a variety of accurate and useful information as could reasonably be expected in a first essay, the writer has recently traversed the whole extent of the lines here traced, writing from personal observation, noticing every thing, on the spot, that seemed to require notice. He has expended in these journies upwards of 200 dollars, and travelled about 1500 miles, using every means in his power to get accurate information; and yet he fears that this little thing, which aims to state so many facts, will be found more defective and inaccurate than he intended it should be. In order to improve and amend the work, each edition will be restricted to a small number of copies, and every succeeding one will be carefully revised and improved, by every suggestion of observation and experience. The writer will be very thankful for every means of expunging errors, supplying omissions, or, in any way of enabling him to make the Directory what it ought to be. If aided, in this way, and patronized, as the undertaking deserves to be, it may assume an improved appearance, and perhaps be accompanied with a Map, and other engravings.

Persons wishing general and minute information concerning the Topography, Geography, and Statistics of the State of New-York, may be referred, the author flatters himself, without vanity, to the new Gazetteer and Geography of this State, published in 1824, by B. D. Packard, bookseller, 71 State-street, Albany, 620 pages octavo, with a new Map, and profiles of the Canals, price 3 dollars, bound. If literary efforts, of this sort, merit any encouragement, Mr. Packard is entitled to every consideration from the public and the trade.

H. G. S.

King-street, Troy, 9 *mo.*, 1824.

A

POCKET GUIDE

FOR

THE TOURIST AND TRAVELLER.

——◆——

Hudson River Steam-Boats. Sept. 1824.

THE Boats of the 'Old Company,' Living-
ston and Fulton, are arranged as below, for 1824,
passage $ 4, between New-York and Albany :—

From New-York.

Sunday,	Chancellor,	at 9 A. M.
Monday,	Richmond,	5 P. M.
Tuesday,	James Kent,	10 A. M.
Wednesday,	Chancellor,	5 P. M.
Thursday,	James Kent,	10 A. M.
Friday,	Richmond,	5 P. M.
Saturday,	James Kent,	5 P. M.

From Albany.

Sunday,	Richmond,	at 9 A. M.
Monday,	James Kent,	9 A. M.
Tuesday,	Chancellor,	10 A. M.
Wednesday,	James Kent,	9 A. M.
Thursday,	Richmond,	10 A. M.
Friday,	James Kent,	9 A. M.
Saturday,	Chancellor,	10 A. M.

The Steam-Boat Olive Branch, ' *Union Line,*'
opposition, fare $ 3 50, 'sails from Jersey City,

for New-York and Albany,' every Tuesday, Thursday, and Saturday, at 10 A. M.; returning, leaves Albany every Sunday, Wednesday, and Friday, at 9 A. M. The Hudson, same line, fare $ 4, leaves New-York every Tuesday and Thursday, at 10 A. M., and every Saturday, at 5 P. M.; and Albany, every Monday, Wednesday, and Friday, at 9 A. M. Another Boat will be in this line in a few days. Sept. 22, 1824.

The *Troy Steam-Boat Company* will soon have one Boat, and next spring two, plying *direct*, between Troy and New-York, *by the way of* ' *Jersey City*,' a perfectly ridiculous farce, even if played ' according to law.'

Besides these Steam-Boats, for passengers, there are extensive associations, engaged in the shipping and forwarding business on the Hudson, connected with those on the Canals, and contracts may be made with them on very advantageous terms, either in New-York, Albany, Troy, or with the Canal forwarding associations.

It appears to be about time for Steam-freighting on the Hudson, for certainty and despatch are highly desirable in commercial operations.

HUDSON RIVER.

Distances between New-York and Albany.

[Measured on the ice.]

NEW-YORK, City, population in 1820, 123,706, now, probably, 133 to 135,000; *City-Hall*, N. lat. 40° 42' 43", W. lon. from Greenwich, England, 73° 59' 46",—from Washington, E. lon. 3° 1' 13", about 18 miles north of Sandy-Hook Light-House and the Ocean,   145

R. [Right] Battery, confluence East and Hudson Rivers, Castle Garden.

L. [Left] shore of the Hudson R., Jersey City, Powles' Hook, New-Jersey.

		Albany Miles
¾	r. Cortlandt-street, Steam Ferry to Jersey City, - - -	144¼
1	r. City-Hall, from which distances are usually reckoned, -	144
1½	r. North Battery, - -	143½
2½	r. State Prison, Greenwich, op. [opposite] Hoboken, New-Jersey,	142½
3	r. Fort Gansevoort, r. Greenwich, Country Seats, - -	142
3½	r. 1 m. from River, United States' Arsenal, - - -	142½
5¼	r. 1 m. from R., Elgin, Botanic Garden, - - - -	139¾
5¾	l. Hamilton Monument, under Palisado Rock, New-Jersey; r. Bloomingdale, - -	139½

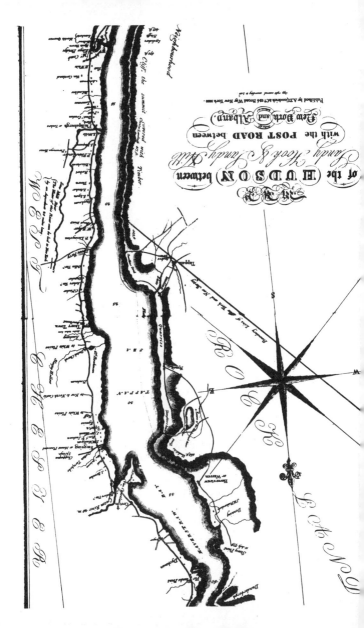

7¼　r. Bloomingdale Lunatic Asylum,　137¼

　8　r. line Military Works, erected
　　　　during late War, extending to
　　　　East River, -　-　-　- 137
Late Lord Courtney.

8⅓　r. Manhattanville, l. Palisadoes 170
　　　　feet, greenstone trap; l. Bull's
　　　　Ferry, -　-　-　-　- 136⅔

　9　r. C. D. Colden, and late Gen. Ha-
　　　　milton,　-　-　-　- 136

10　r. Mount Washington Spring,　- 135
　　　l. Fort Lee, Palisadoes 311 feet.

11　r. Fort Washington, of the Rev.
　　　　War, elevated 238 feet above
　　　　the Hudson,　-　-　- 134

12½　l. Lydicher's Bluffs, 407 feet, ' Eng-
　　　　lish Neighborhood,'　-　- 132½
The Palisadoes extend 20 miles on
　the left, from Hoboken to Tap-
　pan, rising gradually in elevation
　from 20 to 100, and to 550 feet.

13　r. Spyten Duyvel Kill, communi-
　　　　cating with Haerlem River;
　　　　Kingsbridge Marble, and r. 1
　　　　m. Kingsbridge, Stage road,　132
　　　r. Fort Independence, Westchester
　　　　County. Country Seats, along
　　　　the Stage road.
　　　l. Palisadoes, 470 feet to 500 and
　　　　550, along shore, for 10 miles
　　　　northerly.

7¼　r. *Yonkers V.*, or Philipstown, Saw
　　　　Mill Creek, op. Closter Land-
　　　　ing, New-Jersey, -　-　- 127¾
　　　r. Country Seats, on Stage road,

New-York.
Miles.

Albany.
Miles.

21¼	l. New-Jersey and New-York Line, Palisadoes 550 feet, - -	123½
23⅓	Dobb's Ferry, l. Landing and road to Andre's Grave, Tappan, [2½] - - -	121½
26	l. Slote Landing, on lower end, Tappan Bay, - - - -	119
27	r. *Tarrytown*, near which Maj. Andre was taken, - - -	118
29½	l. Nyak, red sand-stone quarries, op. mid. Tappan Bay, - -	115½
32	r. *Sparta V.*, Marble quarries, op. the Hook Landing, - -	113
	l. 1¼ m. Hackensack pond, source Hackensack River of New-Jersey.	
33	r. *Mount Pleasant V.*, or Sing Sing,	112
34	r. Teller's Point, op. mouth Croton R.; l. Verdrietege Hook, 668 feet above tide Water, - -	111
35	r. Croton, Gen. Van Cortlandt, -	110
36	l. *Haverstraw V.*, on Haverstraw Bay, - - - - -	109
39½	l. Stony Point, S. side Highlands, Rockland Co., - - -	105½
40½	r. Verplanck's Point, Fort Fayette, Cortlandt, Westchester Co., -	104¼
	The Highlands of the Hudson, or Matteawan Mountains, are decidedly primitive, the geological character of the Hudson Valley below.	
43	l. Dunderberg, thunder hill, r. *Peekskill V.*, Westchester Co.,	102
44	Horse Race, - - - -	101
45½	r. Anthony's Nose, Philipstown,	

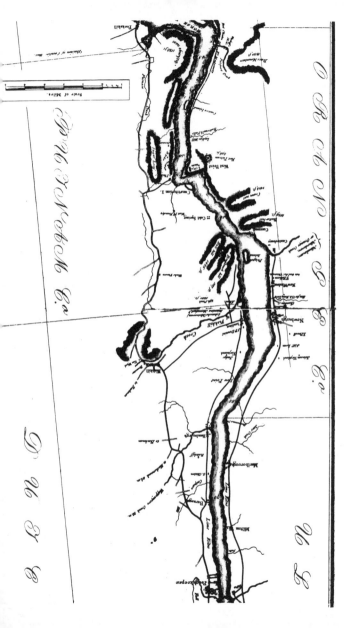

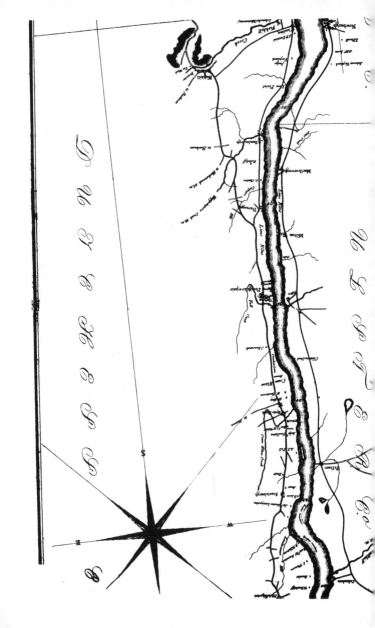

	Putnam Co.; l. Forts Clinton and Montgomery, - -	$99\frac{1}{2}$
	l. Bare Mountain, Cornwall, Orange County.	
50	l. Buttermilk Falls, Cornwall, - -	95
51	r. Sugar Loaf Mountain, 866 feet, Philipstown, Putnam Co., -	94
$52\frac{1}{2}$	l. *West-Point*, U. S. Military Academy, 188 feet, l. Fort Putnam, 598, - - - -	$92\frac{1}{2}$
	r. Pleasant Valley.	
$53\frac{1}{2}$	r. Constitution Island, and r. 2 m. West-Point Foundry, - -	$91\frac{1}{2}$
56	l. Crow's Nest, 1418 ft.; r. Cold-Spring V. and Landing, - -	89
57	r. Bull Hill, 1486 ft., and Breakneck, 1181 ft., Philipstown, -	88
	l. Butter Hill, 1520 ft., Cornwall.	
	l. Putnam Rock, thrown from summit Butter Hill, in June, 1778.	
	l. Cornwall Landing.	
$58\frac{1}{2}$	r. Pollopell Island, l. Canterbury and Moordenar's Kill, - -	$86\frac{1}{2}$
$59\frac{1}{2}$	l. Late Gen. J. Clinton, - -	$85\frac{1}{2}$
60	l. New Windsor V., and Bay, Orange Co., - - -	85
$60\frac{3}{4}$	l. Chambers' Creek, r. mouth Fishkill, Duchess Co., and r. $\frac{1}{2}$ m. Beacon Hill, 1658 ft., - -	$84\frac{1}{4}$
$61\frac{1}{2}$	l. *Newburgh V.*, a half-shire of Orange Co., 2670 inhabitants,	$83\frac{1}{2}$
	r. *Fishkill*, or De Wint's Landing; r. $\frac{1}{4}$ m. Matteawan Cotton Factory, near which is the Grand Sachem, Beacon Hill.	

☞ Valley of the Hudson, along the
    river, transition, northward of here
    to Waterford.

65	r. Low Point, or Carthage, Fish-kill, Duchess Co., - -	80
68	r. New-Hamburgh, Wappinger's Creek, - - - -	77
69½	l. Marleborough, Lime Kilns, Ulster Co.,	75½
70	r. Late Gov. George Clinton, -	75
71	r. Barnegat, Lime Kilns, - -	74
72½	l. Milton, Marleborough, [*Half-Way Place,*] - -	72½
75½	r. Poughkeepsie Landings, 1 mile from the Village, - - -	69½
76	r. 1 m. *Poughkeepsie Village*, cap. Duchess Co., population 2700,	69
	l. New Paltz, horse boat Ferry.	
81	r. Dr. Allen's Academy, Country Seats along Stage road, - -	64
81½	r. Hyde Park, Crom Elbow Creek,	63½
82	r. Late Dr. Bard, - - -	64
83	r. A. S. Pell, (and Country Seats along the R. to near Hudson,)	62
84	l. Pelham, New Paltz, - -	61
86	r. Gen. Lewis, Landing, and 1 m. Staatsberg, - - -	59
	Esopus Meadows, 3 m. northward.	
	l. Shawangunk Mountain, and Mombackus, or Indian Face.	
88	r. R Tillotson, - - - -	57
88½	r. Rev. Mr. Garretson, - -	57½
90½	l. Mouth Wallkill, Esopus Landing, l. 4 miles Kingston V.,	54½
91	r. Rhinebeck Landings, - -	54
97	r. Gen. Armstrong, - - -	48

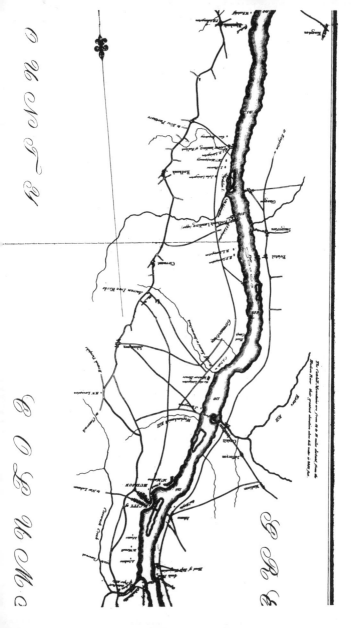

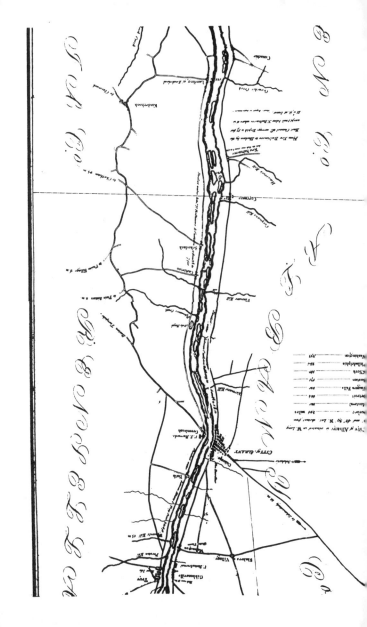

New-York. Miles.		Albany. Miles.
98	r. *Redhook Lower Landing*, J. R. Livingston, - - - -	47
98½	r. Mrs. Montgomery, - - -	46½
99	r. Magdalen Islands, J. Livingston,	46
100	l. Glasgow, r. P. H. Livingston, Saw Kill, - - - -	45
101	r. *Redhook Upper Landing*, J. H. Livingston, Duchess Co., -	44
102	l. Saugerties, Ulster County, Esopus Creek, - - - -	43
103	r. Clermont, seat late Chancellor Livingston, Columbia Co., -	42
	l. Bristol. Flats in the middle of the R. Kaatsbergs, l. 13 to 15 miles.	
107	r. East Camp, Germantown, -	38
	l. Pine-Orchard House, plainly seen from the River, for some miles, distant 12 to 8 miles.	
110	r. Ancram Creek, Manor-House, late Lord Livingston, - -	35
111¾	r. J. Livingston, Oak Hill, - -	33¼
112	l. *Catskill* dock, Kaatskill, and l. *Catskill V.*, cap. Greene County, 1500 inhabitants, - -	33
	The Kaatsbergs, or Catskill Mountains, on the left, are 8 to 12, and 20 miles distant from the river along here, on which is the Pine-Orchard, 12 miles from Catskill, elevated 3000 ft. Regular Stages, in Summer, twice a day, fare $ 1.	
116	r. Mount Merino, and r. ov. S. Bay, S. Plumb, Prospect Hill, and Becraft's Hill, - - -	29

117 Low Island, 2 miles long; l. late
  Gen. Haight, r. South Bay,
  Hudson, - - - - 28

117½ r. HUDSON, City, cap. Columbia
  County, pop. 3600, - 27½
  r. 3 miles, Claverack V., on the
  Sheffield turnpike.
  l. *Athens*, Greene County, Ferry
  Canal, through Flats.
  These places are within 4 miles of
  the head of Ship Navigation,
  to which, by-and-by, the Canals will be conducted, or, the
  Ship Navigation to the Canals.

121 l. Paddock Point, Fishery; right
  Abram's Creek, R. L. Livings-
  ton, and ¾ m. Columbiaville, 24

125 l. *Coxsackie Landings*, and l. 1 m.
  Coxsackie V., - - - 20

126¼ r. *Kinderhook Landing*, now Stuy-
  vesant, [when any body calls
  it so!] - - - - - 18¾
  r. 5 miles, *Kinderhook V.*

130 l. *New Baltimore V.*, Greene Co.,
  [water to this place 11 ft., tides
  3 to 4½ ft.,] - - - - 15

 ☞ Many Islands, from here to Albany,
  and to Waterford; channel very
  crooked, and variable.

131 l. Haanekrai Kill, Cock-crowing
  Creek, - - - - - 14

132 l. *Coeyman's V.*, Albany Co., - 13

135 r. *Schodac V.* and Landing, Rensselaer Co., - - - - 10

B

New-York.
Miles.

Albany
Miles.

136½   r. *Castleton V.*, and Landing, shoal
waters, 4 to 7 ft. to New-Bal-
timore, and 4½ to 5½ to Albany, and the tides 2 to 4 ft.,
[highest,] -   -   -   -   8½

137   l. Vlamans Kill, Bethlehem, Win-
ne's Bar, late Col. Nichols, -   8

139   r. Hogeberg, or High Hill, Schodac, -   -   -   -   -   6

140   r. Prospect Hill, E. C. Genet,
Greenbush, Dam,   -   -   5

141   l. to 143½, Mills's Island, Bethlehem and Albany, 1½ to -   -   4

142   Overslagh, shoals and sand bars,
difficult navigation, l. Dam,   3
l. Norman's Kill, Van Rensselaer's
Mills, Bethlehem.

145   ALBANY, City, cap. State, and of
Albany County, N. lat. 42° 39′,
W. lon. 73° 13′, from Greenwich, Eng.; 12630 inhabitants;
tides, 2 to near 4 feet.
l. The Capitol, or State House, elevated 130 feet, 144 miles from
the City-Hall, New-York, 145
from the Battery.
Albany and Greenbush Ferry.
r. ov. R., *Greenbush*, Rensselaer
Co., turnpike to New-Lebanon
Spring, 25 miles.
r. on River Hill, Mount Madison,
U. S. Barracks, Greenbush
Farm.
The *Erie Canal*, enters the Hudson in Albany, at the head of

the *Albany Basin*, 362 miles
E. of Buffalo, and 72 S. of
Whitehall, by the Canals, for
which see ERIE CANAL and
CHAMPLAIN CANAL: but the
Sloop Navigation, to Troy, is
very nearly as good as to Albany, and the Dam and Sloop
Lock, upper part of Troy, are
intended to make it as good to
Lansingburgh and Waterford,
to which places I continue the
line of Navigation by the Hudson.

☞ *Note.*—The distances, here given,
fall considerably short of those
in the channel of the river, or the
navigation distances, which may
be assumed at little short of 160
miles, between New-York and Albany.

l. Albany Basin, 4000 feet in length,
having a Sloop Lock at its
lower extremity, and Lock
No. 1, of the Erie Canal, or
Grand Junction, at its upper
extremity: it is 80 to 300 feet
wide, water 10 to 15 feet deep.

Above
Albany
by
water.

145½ l. State Arsenal, head of the Basin,
and Upper Ferry, to Bath, ½

r. *Bath V.*, Greenbush, road to
Sand Lake, 10 miles.

146   l. Gen. Van Rensselaer, Manor-
House of Rensselaerwyck, the
‘ Patroon,’   -   -   -   1

New-York. Miles.		Above Albany by water. Miles.
146¾	Fish-House Bar, - - - -	1¾
148	Van Buren's Bar; water, on these bars, hardly 4 feet at lowest,	3
149½	r. Wynants Kill, Mills, Factories, Troy Iron and Nail Works,&c.	4½
	Washington Bar, l. Village Washington, Watervliet.	
151½	r. Poesten Kill, Mills, &c. - -	6½
	l. United States' Arsenal, Watervliet, Village of Gibbonsville.	
152	r. Troy, City, cap. Rensselaer Co., 5264 inhabitants, - -	7
	Two Ferries, river 900 feet in width, usual tides 1 foot.	
	l. *Gibbonsville*, Basins, Hanks's Bell Foundry.	
	l. *West Troy*, Basin, Side-Cut to Erie Canal, 2 Locks, and Weigh Lock, mouth lower Sprout of the Mohawk River.	
	l. Islands in the delta of the Mohawk, to near Waterford.	
153	Dam, and r. Sloop Lock, [connected with Champlain Canal Navigation at Waterford, by a Side-Cut and 3 Locks,] - -	8
	r. Old Bank Place, and Mount Olympus, Troy.	
154¼	l. Middle Sprout of the Mohawk, between Green & Van Schaick Islands, - - - -	9¼
155	r. *Lansingburgh*, 1650 inhabitants,	10
	l. Upper Sprout Mohawk River, Locks and Side-Cut to Canal, ½ mile.	

156   1. *Waterford*, Saratoga Co., popu-
        lation 1000, -   -   -   -   11
      Bridge over the Hudson River, the
        first from the Ocean.
      ☞ Distance, from New-York to
        the Erie Canal, 145¼ miles;
        to the Champlain Canal, at
        Waterford, 156½ ;—or, by the
        Erie Canal, from Albany to
        Juncta, 145½+8½=154 ;—or,
        through the Side-Cut to Troy,
        152+2¼=154¼.

Erie Canal Packet Boats.

Fare, including board, lodging, and every expense, 4 cents a mile.   Way passengers pay
3 cents a mile, exclusive of board, &c., and 37½
cents for dinner, 25 cents for breakfast, or sup-
per, and 12½ cents for lodging.

These Packets are drawn by 3 horses, having
relays every 8, 10, to 12 miles, and travel day
and night, making about 80 miles every 24
hours.   They are ingeniously and well con-
structed, (though there is yet room for some im-
provement,) have accommodations for about 30
passengers, furnish good tables, and a wholesome
and rich fare, and have very attentive, civil, and
obliging captains and crews.   It is a very pleasant, cheap, and expeditious mode of travelling,
where you have regular meals, pretty quiet rest,
after a little experience, say of the first night ;
and find the time pleasantly employed, in con-

versation, and the variety of incidents, new topics, stories, and the constantly varying scenery. The bustle of new comers, and departing passengers, with all the greetings and adieus, help to diversify the scene, and to make most persons *seem* to get along quite as fast as was anticipated.   I found it so, while twice traversing the whole extent of the Erie Canal Navigation, taking notes for this little thing, which, I hope, *every body* will find an useful, if not an agreeable companion.

Between *Albany* and *Schenectady*, 28¼ miles, a day is employed, there being so many Locks to pass: but every person is well compensated for the time and expense, of, at least, one trip, passing 27 Locks, 2 Aqueducts, and an interesting variety of natural scenery.

A Packet leaves *Albany* every day, Sundays excepted, at 7 A. M., and meets the Schenectady Packet at 2 P. M., between the 2 Aqueducts, passing Alexander's Bridge and the Upper Aqueduct, about 4 P. M., and arrives at Schenectady about 6, in time for the Utica Packets. Another Packet leaves *Schenectady* every morning at 9, Sundays excepted, passes the Upper Aqueduct about 10, and arrives at *Albany* about 8 P. M.

Westward, from *Schenectady*, a Packet departs every morning and evening, at 7 o'clock, and runs through to *Utica*, 79½ miles, passing 26 Locks in 24 hours, arriving in season for the Packets for Rochester.   Going eastward, the Packets leave *Utica*, in the same order, for *Schenectady*.

From *Utica*, westward, 2 daily lines depart at 7, morning and evening, for *Rochester*, 160 miles,

passing 25 Locks, and arrive in 46 hours; returning, from *Rochester*, in the same order and
time, to *Utica*.

From *Rochester*, westward, to Brockway, or
Brockport, there was a Packet, in July, twice a
day, 19¾ miles, connected with the lines eastward, as to hours of arrival and departure: but
the Canal will be open, this autumn, to *Lockport*,
63 miles from Rochester, when Packets will run
through that distance, without a Lock, probably
between the rising and setting of the sun. I
passed the Long Level, 69½ miles, in July, from
the Lock in Frankfort, to that at its W. extremity, by one day's sun, besides breakfasting on
shore, at Utica, and changing Packets. Would
it not be well, next season, to run each Packet
through the whole extent of the navigation?

The Packet-Boat Companies have extensive
connexions with the lines of Stages, the hours of
arrival and departure of which are so arranged
that there is little detention, in passing, in almost
any direction, at any of the considerable Villages,
from the Canal line. These Packets also carry
the Mails.

———

On the Northern, or *Champlain Canal*, there
is one Packet, plying between Fort-Edward and
Whitehall, regulated, in its trips, conformably to
those of the Champlain Steam-Boat, for which
see below, and Fort-Edward, under *Champlain
Canal*.

The *Lake Champlain Steam-Boat* leaves
Whitehall, for St. John's, every Thursday and
Saturday, at 2 P. M., touching at all the inter-
mediate places; fare, through, 8 dollars; and

the same returning, when it leaves St. John's, Lower Canada, every Monday and Friday, at 8 A. M.

From Whitehall to Ticondero-

ga, -	-	-	-	-	24 miles,	$1 50
Crown Point,	-	-	-	39 ——	2 50
Basin Harbor,	-	-	-	51 ——	3 00
Essex, -	-	-	-	61 ——	3 50
Burlington, -	-	-	-	75 ——	4 00
Port Kent, -	-	-	-	91 ——	4 00
Plattsburgh,*	-	-	-	99 ——	5 00
Chazy, -	-	-	-	114 ——	6 00
Champlain, Rouse's Point,		-	126 ——	6 50
St. John's, Lower Canada,		-	150 ——	8 00

From St. John's to La Prairie, by Stage, 18 miles, thence by water, regular Packet-Boat, 9 miles, = 27, to Montreal. There are regular lines of Stages, between Albany and Montreal. From Montreal to Quebec, Steam-Boat, 180 miles; fare and regulations, not known. Who will inform me?

On *Lake George*, the Steam-Boat leaves Caldwell, for Ticonderoga, every Tuesday and Saturday, at 7 A. M.; returning, leaves Ticonderoga at 2 P. M., and reaches Caldwell at 8, the same evening. This arrangement enables persons going on Lake Champlain, either way, to take a view of Lake George.

* See note to Ogdensburgh, for a Stage, under ' Steam-Boat on Lake Ontario.'

Steam Boat on Lake Ontario.

This Boat leaves *Niagara River*, at 3 P. M.,
Sept. 1, 10, 18, and 27th,
and Oct. 6 and 15th.

Genesee River, at 4 P. M.,
Sept. 2, 11, 19, and 28th,
and Oct. 7 and 16th.

Sacket's Harbor, at 9 P. M.,
Sept. 3, 12, 20, and 29th,
and Oct. 8 and 17th.

Returning, leaves *Ogdensburgh*,* at 9 P. M.,
Sept. 4, 13, 21, and 30th,
and Oct. 9 and 18th.

Sacket's Harbor, at 4 P. M.,
Sept. 6, 14, and 23d, and
Oct. 2 and 11th.

Genesee River, Sept. 8, 16,
and 25th, and Oct. 4 and
13th.

Passage, the same each way, Cabin, Niagara
R. to Genesee R., $3; Forward Cabin, $2;
Deck, $1 50:—Genesee R. to Sacket's H.,
Cabin, $5; Forward Cabin, $3; Deck, $2:—
Sacket's H. to Ogdensburgh, Cabin, $5; For-
ward Cabin, $3; Deck, $2.

The Steam-Boat Enterprise, on CAYUGA
LAKE, makes a trip every day, from Ithaca to
the CAYUGA BRIDGE, and back—fare, each way,

---

* A regular Stage, once a week, leaves Ogdensburgh
on every Saturday morning, and arrives at Plattsburgh
on Monday, in time for the Steam-Boat going south;
it leaves Plattsburgh, for Ogdensburgh, every Wednesday, at 7 A. M.

1 dollar; for breakfast and dinner, 25 cents—
tea, 18. It is a good Boat, well found, and the
trip is one of the pleasantest in the western
country. Distances, and price of passage, going
up the Lake, charged in the same proportion
returning. Passengers are taken, and landed, at
both ends of the Bridge, and at all the places on
the Lake. See *Montezuma*, p. 39.

From the Bridge, Miles.			Fare.
6	l. Springport, formerly Union Springs, - - -	-	$0 25
10	l. Levana, Town of Ledyard,	-	0 37½
12	l. Aurora, Aurora, - -	-	0 37½
19	r. Sheldrake Point, Ovid,	-	0 50
21	r. Kidder's Ferry, Ovid, -	-	0 50
29	r. Frog Point, Covert, -	-	0 75
35	l. Ludlowville, Lansing, -	-	0 87½
42	Port l'Orient, Head of the Lake, - - -	-	1 00
44	ITHACA, Village, by Stage, fare 12½ cents, = -	-	1 12½

Stages, connected with the Boat, are so arranged as to arrive and depart in season for it,
between Montezuma, Geneva, Canandaigua, Auburn, Owego, and most parts of the country;
fare, 4 cents a mile. The Ithaca and Catskill
line of Stages, 4 times a week, fare 4 cents a
mile, runs through in 2½ days, passing through
the principal Villages in Greene, Delaware,
Chenango, Tompkins, and Broome Counties.
Leaves Ithaca Sunday, Tuesday, Thursday, and
Friday, and Catskill same days.

RATES OF TOLL ON THE CANALS. 1824.

On *Packet Boats,* or Boats made and used chiefly for the carriage of persons, 6 *cents per mile of their passage.*

On *Boats,* made and used chiefly for the transportation of property, on each ton of their capacity, 1 *mill per mile.*

On *Salt,* 5 *mills per ton per mile,* [7 barrels, of 5 bushels each, or 40 bushels in bulk, being a ton.]

On *Gypsum,* or Plaster of Paris, 5 *mills per ton per mile.*

On *Flour, Meal,* and *all kinds of Grain, salted Provisions, Pot and Pearl Ashes,* 1½ *cent per ton per mile.*

On *Merchandize,* 3 *cents per ton per mile.*

On *Timber,* squared and round, 1 *cent per hundred solid feet per mile.*

On *Boards, Plank,* and *Scantling,* reduced to inch measure, and on all *Siding, Lath,* and other *Sawed Stuff,* less than 1 inch thick, 1 *cent per thousand feet per mile.*

On *Shingles,* 2 *mills per thousand per mile.*

On *Brick, Sand, Lime, Iron-Ore,* and *Stone,* 5 *mills per ton per mile.*

On *Rails,* and *Posts for Fencing,* 3 *cents per thousand per mile.*

On *Wood,* for fuel, 1 *cent per cord per mile.*

☞ All *Fuel,* to be used in the manufacture of Salt, to pass free.

On *Staves* and *Heading,* for *pipes,* 1 *cent per thousand per mile.*

On *Staves* and *Heading,* for *hogsheads,* 7 *mills per thousand per mile.*

On *Staves* and *Heading*, for *barrels*, or less,
 5 *mills per thousand per mile.*
On *Household Furniture*, *Iron Ware*, of *Domestic Manufacture*, and on all articles *not enumerated*, 1 *cent per ton per mile.*

Tolls may be paid at any of the Collectors' Offices, for any distance, at the option of the Master, taking a Clearance for that distance.

***

PRICES OF TRANSPORTATION.

These, of course, are subject to variation. The rates fixed by the principal Transportation Companies, in which great capitals are employed, are, on the Canals, on *Merchandize*, 2 cents per ton per mile; or, they guarantee, at 5 cents per ton per mile, including the Tolls. On *Produce*, such as grain, provisions, &c. transportation 1½ cent per mile, or 3 cents including the Tolls.

Passengers, in these Boats, pay 1 to 1½ cent per mile, exclusive of board.

These Companies are perfectly responsible, consisting of merchants, and men of business and enterprise, some individuals of which reside in all the principal Cities, Towns, Villages, and business-places in this State, and in the commercial and trading Towns of the interior of the United States. They contract for the conveyance of all sorts of property, through any part, or the whole extent, of the long lines of commercial intercourse in this State, and from and to most parts of the interior of the Union, guaranteeing its safe and expeditious delivery. Their Boats are covered, and some of them travel day and night, making about 50 to 60 miles every 24 hours.

I am sorry to see that these great Companies are making such a monopoly of the Transportation busines, driving off the small capitalists, and the many hundreds of poor and industrious men, who are striving to support themselves and families, by this new species of the Carrying Trade. They will do it, however; for wealth will have its own way; and power will beget power, and strengthen itself—a tendency that we, little, weak men, may deplore, but ought always to be aware of, and, so far as may be, to guard against.

COLLECTORS' OFFICES, AND COLLECTORS, ON THE ERIE CANAL.

Albany,	-	-	J. B. Staats.
West-Troy,	-	-	J. Burrows.
Schenectady,	-	-	J. Myers.
Little Falls,	-	-	S. Lansing.
Utica,	-	-	S. Williams.
Rome,	-	-	B. B. Hyde.
Syracuse,	-	-	—— Colvin.
Montezuma,	-	-	R. Matson.
Lyons,	-	-	J. Adams.
Palmyra,	-	-	—— Colt.
Rochester,	-	-	C. A. Van Slyck.
Brockport,	-	-	J. Seymour.

ON THE CHAMPLAIN CANAL.

Waterford,	-	-	F. Livingston.
Northumberland,	· Saratoga		
Guard Gates,'	-	-	J. Olmsted.
Fort Miller,	-	-	S. T. Shepherd.
Fort Edward,	-	-	T. Eddy.
Fort Anne,	-	-	L. Hastings.
Whitehall,	·	-	W. B. Van Benthuysen.

C

Amount of Tolls, from April 15, to July 31, 1824, 3½ months, $146,738 17, probably $200,000 to September 1, 1824. The duties on Salt, May 1, to July 31, 3 months, amounted to $34,242 55; and on sales at auction, for Canal Fund, same period, to $60,192 35: total, from these sources of revenue, ascertained, for about 1 quarter year, or say an average of the whole, $241,173 7. The income, for sales of lands, on bonds and debts, belonging to the *Canal Fund*, [which, on November 30, 1823, amounted to $55,071 22, exclusive of the whole value of the Canals,] not included in this statement. Annual interest on the Canal debt, $380,323 55, about one fourth less than the income of the Canal Fund.

Total cost of the Canals, to Sept. 1, 1824, including money borrowed this year, but exclusive of interest on the Canal loans, $8,061,735 46. The Erie Canal is now completed to Lockport, 331 miles, leaving only 31 miles unfinished.

ERIE CANAL.

Length, from Albany to Buffalo, - miles 362
Number of Locks, on main trunk, - 83
Whole Lockage, - - - feet 688
Declivity, from Buffalo to Rochester, feet 4

Whole amount of rise and fall, - feet 692
Elevation of Lake Erie, above tide-water of
   Hudson River, at low water in summer,
   568 feet; but subject to some variation,
   at Lake Erie and in the Hudson.

From Albany to Schenectady, 28½ miles, Feet.
   27 Locks, all ascending, - - rise 226
From Schenectady to Utica, 79½ miles,
   26 Locks, all ascending, - - rise 198
From Utica to Seneca River, Montezuma,
   [45 feet below Utica,] 96 miles, 9 Locks;
   whole Lockage, rise and fall, - - 79
From Seneca River to Buffalo, 158 miles,
   21 Locks, all ascending, - - rise 185
      Total—length, 362 miles, 83 Locks,
      688 feet Lockage.

Albany.   Buffalo.
Miles.   **ERIE CANAL.**   Miles.

ALBANY, City, capital of the State,
   N. lat. 42° 39', W. lon. 73° 13',
   from Greenwich, England.—Population, 12,630, - - - 362

The *Albany Basin*, embracing the W.
   side of Hudson River, is about 4000
   feet in length, in front of the City,
   from the foot of Hamilton-Street,
   near the Steam-Boat Dock, to the
   State Arsenal, where it communi-
   cates with the Canal by Lock No. 1,
   3 Qrs. of a mile N. E. of the Capitol
   or State House.

Lock No. 1, rise 12 feet, and the
    Little Basin, Albany.

L. [Left] State Arsenal.

R. [Right] Albany Upper Ferry;
    over river, *Bath* Village.

$\frac{1}{3}$ l. Manor House of Rensselaerwyck,
    'Patroon,' Gen. Van Rensse-
    laer, Watervliet, - - - 361$\frac{2}{3}$

$1\frac{1}{2}$ Lock No. 2, rise 11 feet, Water-
    vliet, [to Lower Aqueduct,] - 360$\frac{1}{2}$

4   l. The Albany & Troy 'Half-Way
    House,' or Houses? - - 358

5   r. *Washington V.*, and road to
    Shaker Village, Watervliet, - 357

$5\frac{1}{2}$ r. *United States' Arsenal, Gibbons-
    ville*, and Basins, Watervliet, - 356$\frac{1}{2}$

$6\frac{1}{4}$ r. *West Troy*, Basin, Side-Cut, op-
    posite Troy, 2 Locks & Weigh
    Lock, - - - - - 355$\frac{3}{4}$

    l. Turnpike to Schenectady, 13
    miles; Shaker Village, 6.

$7\frac{1}{4}$ l. V. D. Oothout, $\frac{1}{4}$ m. above Oo-
    thout's Basin, - - - 354$\frac{1}{4}$

$8\frac{1}{2}$ *Juncta*, or the Junction, where
    the Erie receives the Cham-
    plain Canal, by a Navigable
    Feeder from the Mohawk, be-
    low which there is a Basin
    and 2 Locks, Nos. 3 and 4,
    2 of the '*Nine Locks*,' Nos.
    3 to 11, in about a half mile,
    rise 78 feet, - - - - 353$\frac{1}{2}$

    r. From Juncta, by Champlain Ca-
    nal, to Waterford, 2 miles.

    l. A. G. Lansing, at Lock No. 6.

Albany. Miles.		Buffalo. Miles.
9	Lock No. 12, rise 8 feet, - -	353
9¼	The ' *Three Locks*,' Nos. 13, 14, 15, rise 26 feet, opposite *Cahoos Bridge*, - - -	352¾
9½	The ' *Two Locks*,' Nos. 16, 17, rise 18 feet, - - - -	352$\frac{1}{2}$
10	Deep Cutting, 26 feet, 40 rods, transition argillite, - -	352
	r. *Cohoos Falls*, perpendicular descent 78 feet.	
10¼	r. Paper Mill, on Mohawk River,	351¼
10½	The *Four Locks*,' Nos. 18, 19, 20, 21, rise 32 feet, - -	351$\frac{1}{2}$
	r. Wing Dam, and Grist, Saw and Plaster Mill, Watervliet, Albany County.	
12½	*Lower Aqueduct* over Mohawk River, 1188 feet, 26 piers, and abutments of stone, the trunk of wood, S. end Watervliet, -	349$\frac{1}{2}$
12¾	Fonda's Ferry; T. of Halfmoon, Saratoga County, [to Upper Aqueduct,] - - - -	349¼
	l. Mohawk R., r. *Wat Hoix Ridge*.	
14¾	Dunsbagh's Ferry, - - -	347¼
15	*Wat Hoix Gap*, near 40 rods, high walls of graywacke slate, -	347

This singular natural Ravine, so serviceable, was about 80 feet in width at the E. extremity, and 15 at the W., spreading in the middle, for this charming, romantic Basin, high-walled with solid rock. Before this passage was discovered, even our Engineers, full of courage as they were, felt almost

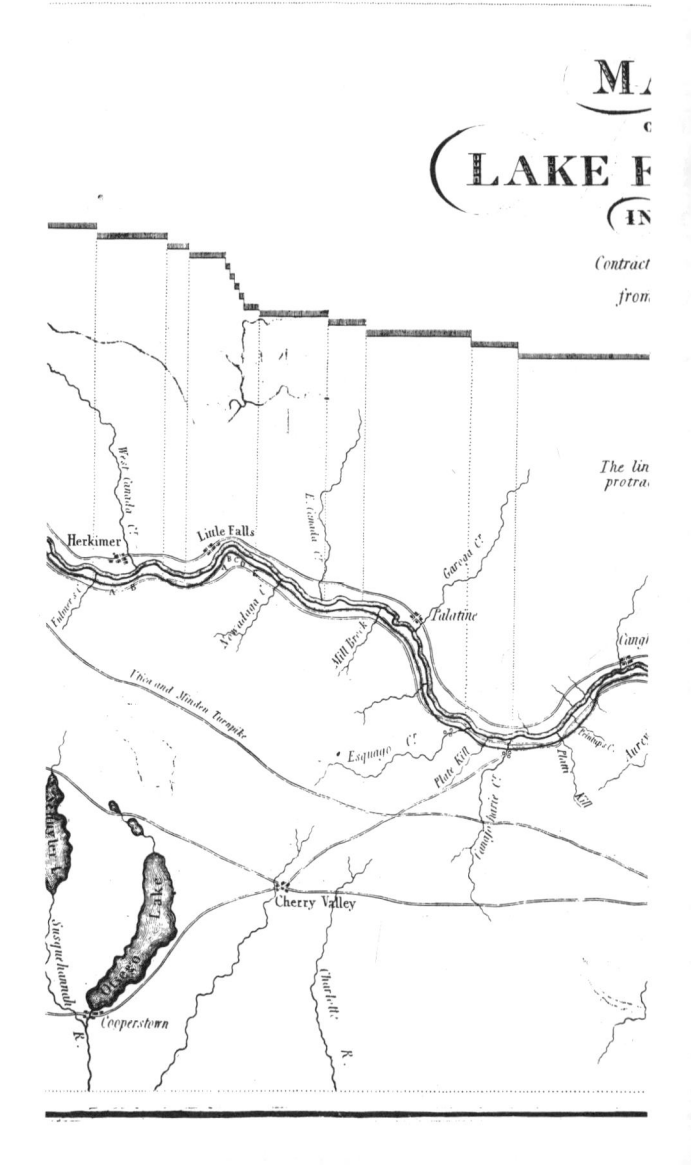

MA[...]

LAKE [...]

IN[...]

Contract[...]

from[...]

The lin[...]
protra[...]

West Canada Cr.

Herkimer   Little Falls

E. Canada Cr.

Nowadaga Cr.

Mill Brook

Palatine

Garoga Cr.

N. B.

E. Canada Cr.

Utica and Minden Turnpike

Esquago Cr.

Esquago Cr.

Plate Kill

Cherry Valley

Plum Kill

Canajoharie Cr.

Canajoharie Cr.

Aure[...]

Cangi[...]

Susquehannah R.

Otsego Lake

Charlotte R.

Cooperstown   R.

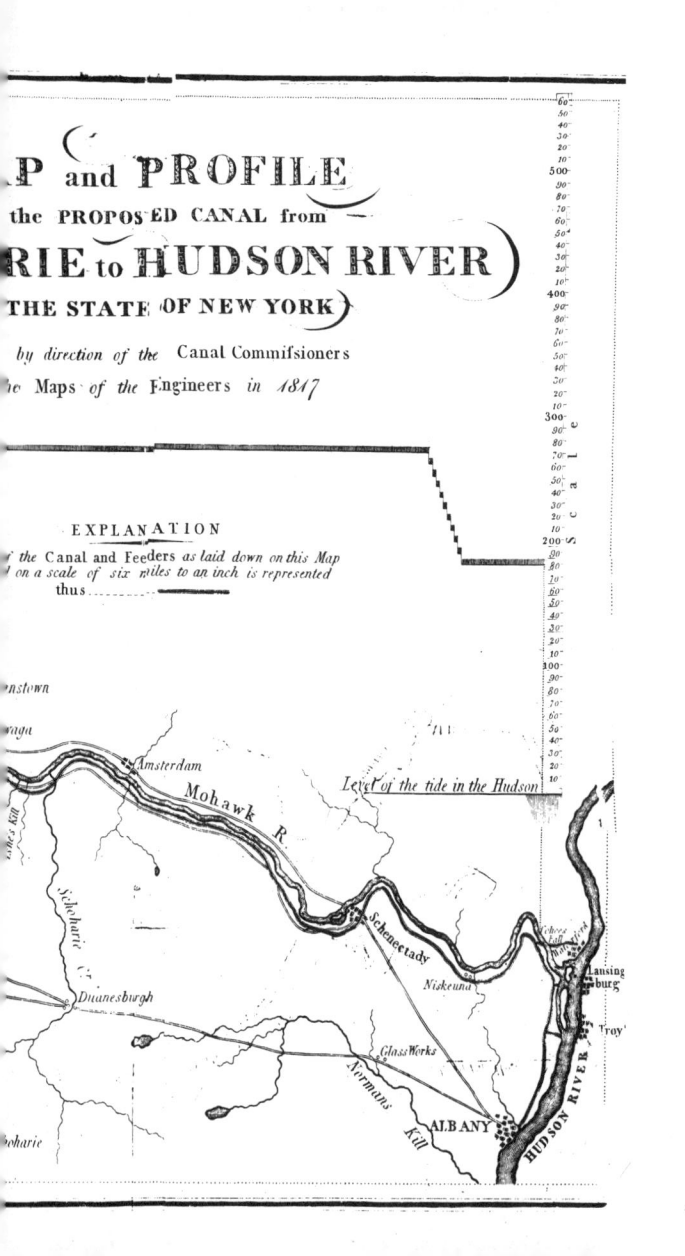

.P and **PROFILE**

the PROPOSED CANAL from

RIE to HUDSON RIVER

THE STATE OF NEW YORK

by direction of the Canal Commissioners

he Maps of the Engineers in 1817

EXPLANATION

the Canal and Feeders as laid down on this Map
on a scale of six miles to an inch is represented
thus..........

Level of the tide in the Hudson

Mohawk R.

Amsterdam

Schoharie

Duanesburgh

Schenectady

Niskeuna

GlassWorks

Normans Kill

ALBANY

HUDSON RIVER

Troy

Lansingburg

Cohoes Falls

nstown

aga

oharie

dismayed. They had examined,
and re-examined, every inch of
the S. shore of the river, rock-
bound and precipitous, and here
first conceived the idea of twice
crossing the Mohawk.

l. 80 rods, *Wat Hoix Rapid*, in
    Mohawk R., 10 feet descent,
    called by the Indians the
    ' *White Horse*,' or *Evil Spirit.*

17   Fort's Ferry, and old road from Al-
      bany to Ballston Spa, -   - 345

18   Lock No. 22, rise 7 feet,   -   - 344

19   Vischer's Ferry, -   -   -   - 343

     l. 3 m. ov. R., Shaker Village, Wa-
      tervliet.

$20\frac{1}{2}$ l. Rock ' *Young Engineer*,' deep
      cutting, 32 feet, transition ar-
      gillite; [deepest on the Ca-
      nal,]   -   -   -   - $341\frac{1}{2}$

$21\frac{1}{2}$ Lock No. 23, rise 7 feet,   -   - $340\frac{1}{2}$

$22\frac{1}{2}$ Lock No. 24, rise 7 feet,   -   - $339\frac{1}{2}$

$24\frac{1}{2}$ *Upper Aqueduct* over Mohawk R.,
      748 feet, 16 piers, 25 feet above
      the river, 3 Locks, Nos. 25, 26,
      27, rise 21 feet, -   - $337\frac{1}{2}$

     Below these, a Guard Lock, and
      Feeder of $\frac{1}{2}$ a mile from Mo-
      hawk R., and a high bank, of
      130 feet.

$24\frac{3}{4}$ *Alexander's Bridge*, and Mills, on
      Ballston and Albany turnpike,
      Niskayuna, Schenectady Co., $337\frac{3}{4}$

     r. $10\frac{1}{2}$ miles, Ballston Spa; and $17\frac{1}{2}$
      Saratoga Springs. There is a

Albany, Miles.		Buffalo Miles.
	'Hack,' at this place, and soon will be a regular Stage, for the Springs.	
25	l. High rock, 28 feet, graywacke slate, in Schenectady, - -	337
27½	r. Rope Ferry, on old road over Mohawk River, - - -	334½
28	l. 100 rods, *Union College*, Schenectady, - - - -	334
28½	SCHENECTADY, City, cap. Schenectady County, pop. 2800, -	333½
31¼	Rotterdam Flats, Lock No. 28, rise 8 feet, - - - - -	330¾
32½	Lock No. 29, rise 8 feet; l. Schermerhorn's, - - - -	329½
33	Aqueduct over Plattekill, - -	329
36¼	Lock No. 30, rise 8 feet, - -	325¾
37	r. Putnam's, Rotterdam, - -	325
38½	County line, Schenectady and Montgomery, near Vedder's Ferry,	323½
39½	l. *Flint Hill*, in Florida, Montgomery Co.; calciferous sandrock, - - - - - -	322½
43	The '*Two Locks*,' Nos. 31 and 32, rise 16 feet; Aqueduct and small Pond, Florida, - -	319
45¾	r. Mears's, Florida, Bridge; and over R., *Amsterdam Village*,	316¼
	Aqueduct ov. Chuctenunda Creek.	
47¾	Lock No. 33, rise 8 feet, - -	314¼
49½	Lock No. 34, rise 4 feet; in the Town of Florida, Montgomery County, - - - - -	312½
	r. Fort Hunter, Queen Anne's Chapel, and old Mohawk Castle.	

50½　*Schoharie Creek*, Guard Lock, Horse Rope-Ferry, and Lock No. 35, rise 6 feet, on the W. bank of Schoharie Creek, - 　-　- 311½

52½　l. 'Canal House,' an oddity, Smithtown, Glen, - 　-　-　- 309¾
　　　Ishe's Kill Aqueduct, and Aries Kill Dam and Guard Locks.

55　Voorhees, Lock No. 36, rise 7 feet, in Glen, 　-　-　-　- 307
　　　r. ov. R., ½ m., Caughnawaga; and 4 m. Johnstown.

60¾　Van Voast's Store, Root, 　-　- 301¼
61　Little Aqueduct and Basin; and r. ov. R., Dachsteder's, and Little Nose, - 　-　-　- 301

61¾　l. *Anthony's Nose*, and *Mitchill's Cave*, Root, formerly Canajoharie, - 　-　-　- 300¼
　　　Gneiss Rock, primitive, the first on the Canal.

62½　r. over R., Kanadarox, or Bread Creek, 　-　-　-　- 299½

64　Spraker's, Canajoharie, Dam and Guard Locks, Plattekill, 　- 298

66¾　Lock No. 37, rise 6 feet, *Canajoharie V.* and Creek, Guard Locks, &c. 　-　-　-　- 295¼
　　　There are Stages, on Tuesday and Friday, from this place to Cherry Valley.
　　　r. over River, Palatine Bridge Village, 67 miles from Albany.

67　Root's, and Basin, Canajoharie, 　- 295

69	r. over R., Stone Arabia, Palatine, [4 miles,] - - - -	293
70	Waggoner's, Lock No. 38, rise 7 feet, Guard Locks, Otsquaga Creek, Minden, -	292
70½	l. Fort Plain V., Minden, -	291½
72½	r. Bridge to Palatine, - - l. Devendorf's Hill, Minden.	289½
73½	r. Feeder from Mohawk R., from above the Dam, Lock No. 39, rise 8 feet, - - -	286½
74½	r. Dam across R. for Feeder, timber and brushwood of 42 acres used in making it; Guard Lock, op. St. Johnsville, Oppenheim, - - -	287½
76½	Crous's, Minden, Lock No. 40, rise 8 feet, - - - -	285½
78	r. ov. R., mouth E. Canada Creek,	284
80	Lock No. 41, rise 8 feet, Danube, Herkimer County, - l. Mohawk Castle, Indian Church and Bell, Danube.	282
81	Nowadaga Creek, Dam, Guard Locks, Towpath 400 feet, Danube, - - - -	281
83	Late Gen. Herkimer, slain in the Oriskany battle, - -	279
84	r. Fink's Ferry; l. E. extremity *Fall Hill*, - - -	278
85	Lock No. 42, rise 8 feet, the lower one of the 'Five Locks,' at the Little Falls, - - - Entrance *Fall Hill Ravine*, walls of rock 50 to 150 feet.	277

1. *Fall Hill,* 518 feet above Canal, 712 above the tides of the Hudson R., 288 above the Rome summit, *Long Level* of the Canal, and 144, or 147, above Lake Erie! Scenery a treat,—grand, imposing, and highly picturesque: 'all hands upon deck,' especially from the Ladies' Cabin: we are approaching the Little Falls. What a tremendous, awe-inspiring scene! Nature has moulded her works, here, on a grand scale,—and soon we shall see, as we may even now, that Art has caught the inspiration of the scene, and well seconded her efforts, in giving to it a sublime effect, and a finish truly admirable.

35½   Lock No. 43, rise 8 feet, -   - 276½
Here we leave the Ravine, and have a view, on the right, of the Old Canal and Locks.

36   Locks Nos. 44 and 45, rise 16 feet, bank of the river, -   -   - 276
r. *Little Falls,* of the Mohawk, 42 feet.

Gniess Rock, second primitive tract on the Canal, and the last, going westward.

r. over River, *Little Falls Village,* Herkimer, Town and County.

r. *Aqueduct*, connecting the Old with the Erie Canal, 3 arches, 1 of 70, and 2 of 50 feet each, a Navigable Feeder, and an elegant feature of the Canal. Taken as a whole, the scenery of this Pass, this gorge of the Mohawk, in works of nature and art, is unrivalled on the Canals of this State.

Lock No. 46, rise 8 feet, the upper one of the ' Five Locks,' rise 40 feet in 1 mile.

88¾	Lock No. 47, rise 8 feet, German Flats, - - . -	273¾
91½	Lock No. 48, rise 9 feet, from the Old Canal, German Flats, -	270½
	l. Stone Church, used as a fortress, and Fort Herkimer.	
92½	r. over River, mouth W. Canada Creek, - - - -	269½
93	r. Bridge ov. Mohawk, [and 1 m. *Herkimer V.*] - - -	269
93½	l. The Dug Way; high hill, clay and sand, - - -	268½
94	Bridge ov. R., and road to *Herkimer Village*, - - -	268
94¾	Lock No. 49, rise 8 feet, - -	267¼
95	Lock No. 50, rise 8 feet, Fulmer's Creek Aqueduct, - -	267
96½	Steel's Creek Aqueduct and Feeder, - - -	265½
97	r. Dygert's Dry Dock, - -	265
97½	Lock No. 51, rise 8 feet, -	264½
97¾	Lock No. 52, rise 8 feet, -	264¼

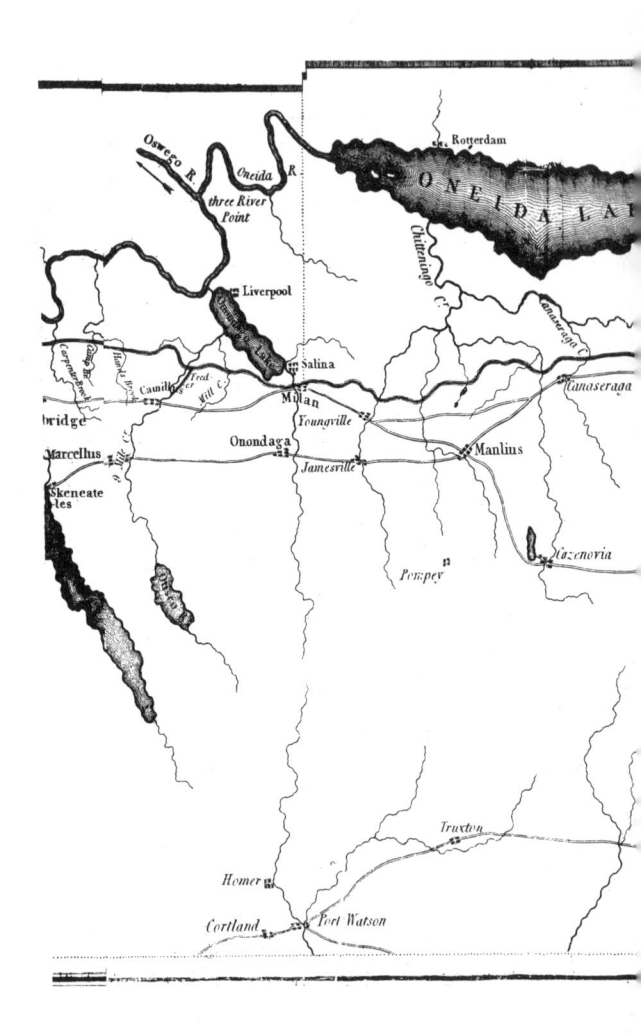

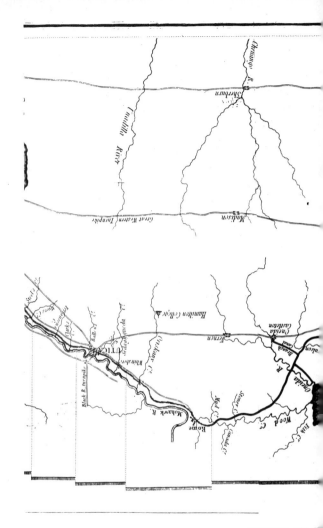

98½   Myers's Creek Aqueduct, and r.
        Frankfort V.   -   -   - 263½

98¾   Lock No. 53, rise 8 feet, Frankfort,
        Herkimer Co.,   -   - 263¼

       The *Long Level*, 69½ miles, commences
       at this Lock, and extends west-
       ward through Utica, Whitestown,
       Rome, Verona, Lenox, Sullivan,
       and Manlius, into Salina, Ononda-
       ga County, terminating there, at
       Lock 54, 3 Qrs. of a mile E. of
       Syracuse.

105   Ferguson's Creek Aqueduct, Frank-
        fort,   -   -   -   - 257

106   Clark's Creek Aqueduct, 4 arches;
        T. of Utica, Oneida Co.,   - 256
      r. Starch Factory and Saw-mill.

108   UTICA V., Utica, Oneida Coun-
       ty, pop. in 1823, 4017, 400
       houses,   .   .   . 160   254
      r. Bridge over the Mohawk,
       road to Deerfield and the
       Black River country, by
       Trenton and W. Canada
       Creek Falls, 15 miles.
      l. 4 m. *New Hartford V.* and
       Hamilton College, 10 m.
      ☞ Utica is a kind of *third-shire*
       of Oneida Co., though not of
       the County Courts, which are
       holden in *but two* places; but
       it has a Court-House, and
       terms of the Supreme, and of
       the U. S. Circuit Court, for
       the Northern District of New-
       York, and the Clerk's Office.
      There are Stages, from Utica,
       in all directions, which will be
       noticed, when I can do it with

Albany. Miles.	Utica. Miles.		Rochester. Miles.	Buffalo. Miles.
		accuracy, as well as the best Public Houses. The new Mill, here, merits the notice of ingenious mechinists, and many property-holders.		
111¼	3¼	Sadaquada Creek Aqueduct, Whitestown, . .	156¾	250¾
	3½	r. late Judge White, first settler.		
112	4	*Whitesborough V.*, a *half-shire* of Oneida County, Whitestown, . .	156	250
		r. Ferguson's Dry Dock.		
114¾	6¾	Oriskany Creek, . .	153¼	247¼
115	7	*Oriskany Village*, Whitestown, . .	153	247
123	15	Mansion House, Rome; r. ov. Old Canal, *Rome V.*, another *half-shire*, . .	145	239
123¾	16	Wood Creek Feeder, Rome, r. United States' Arsenal, on Old Canal, Rome.	144½	238½
126	18	Wood Creek, and Old Canal, Rome, . .	148	236
130	22	Smith's, Verona, .	138	232
136	28	l. *Verona Glass Works*, Loomis's, .	132	226
139	31	*Oneida Creek*, Verona and Lenox line, . .	129	223
142	34	l. *Lenox Furnace*, Basin and Landing. Madison Co., .	126	220
144	36	*Canastota V.*, Creek and Basin, Lenox, .	124	218
148	40	*New Boston V.*, Sullivan, Madison Co., .	120	214
152	44	*Chitteningo Creek*, Aqueduct, Basin, and Feeder, Sullivan, .	116	210
		l. Side Cut to *Chitteningo V.*, 1½ m, 4 Locks, rise 6 feet each.		

D

Albany. Miles.	Utica. Miles.		Rochester. Miles.	Buffalo. Miles.
		A twice a week line of Stages runs from Carey's, Chittenin- go Village, to Cortlandt Co., on Wednesday and Saturday mornings, reaches Cortlandt V. same evening, and returns on Mondays and Thursdays.		
160	52	*Manlius Landing,* Manlius, Onondago Co., . . .	108	202
		l. 4 miles, *Manlius Village.*		
163	55	l. Side-Cut to *Orville,* T. of Manlius, .	105	199
168¼	60¼	Lock No. 54, fall 10 feet, W. end *Long Level,* Salina, no- ticed at Lock No. 53,	99¾	193¾
		Lock No. 55, fall 10 feet, or 20 at the 2 Locks, where the water is passed around, and supplies a saw-mill on the right.		
169	61	*Syracuse V.,* and Salt Works, Town of Salina, . .	99	193
		l. 5 miles, Onondago Court- House, Village.		
		r. Side-Cut to *Salina,* 1¼ m., Salt Works.		
		A small Packet Boat plies be- tween these places, fare, each way, 12½ cents.		
169¼	61¼	Lock No. 56, fall 6 feet, in Salina, . : .	98¾	192¾
170½	62½	Lock No. 57, rise 6 feet, Sa- lina, . .	97½	191½
171	63	*Geddes V.,* and Salt Works, Salina, . . .	97	191
		r. *Onondaga Lake,* Salina.		
177	69	*Otisco,* or 9 Mile Creek, Aque- duct, Lock No. 58, rise 11 feet, . . .	91	185
183	75	*Canton V.,* Camillus, [Half Way V. between Albany and Buffalo,] .	85	179

Albany. Miles.	Utica. Miles.		Rochester Miles.	Buffalo. Miles.
189	81	*Jordan V.*, Camillus, Onondaga Co., Lock No. 59, fall 11 feet, Aqueduct ov. Skaneateles Creek, . .	79	173
		l. *Skaneateles V.*, 9 miles; no regular conveyance.		
		l. 2 miles, *Elbridge V.*		
195	87	*Weed's Basin*, and *Middleport*, Brutus, Cayuga Co.,	73	167
		l. 7 m., AUBURN, cap. Cayuga County. Regular Stage, connected with Packet Boats, fare 50 cents.		
198	90	*Bucksville*, Mentz, Lock No. 60, fall 9 feet, Aqueduct over Owasco Creek, .	70	164
		Here are Dry Docks, & large Boat Houses, for building and repairing.		
202½	94½	Lock No. 61, fall 9 feet, .	65½	159½
204	96	*Montezuma*, Mentz, Cayuga Co., Lock No. 62, fall 7 feet, to Seneca River, . .	64	158
		Bridge Towpath, over Rivers and Cayuga Marshes, near 3 miles westward, Junius, Seneca County.		
		r. 1–third of a mile, Montezuma Salt Works, Turnpike Bridge, Causeway, and Prospect Hill, commanding an elegant & extensive view.		
		This place is on the E. border of the great *Cayuga Marshes*, through which the Canal is carried, and of the Seneca River. When these marshes are well drained, here will be the garden of the State.		

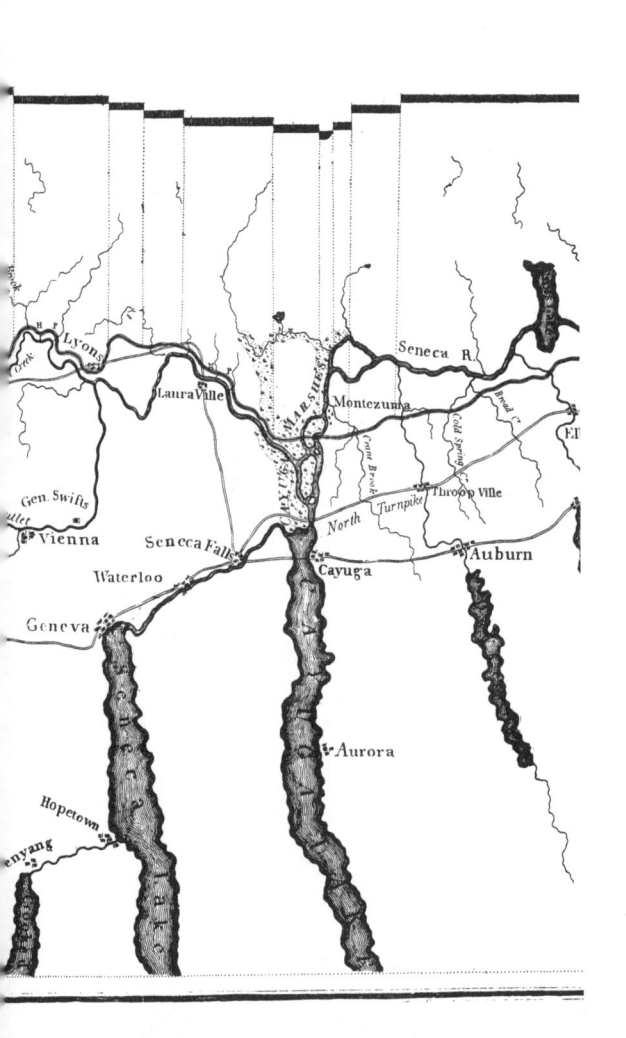

Albany. Miles.	Utica. Miles.		Rochester. Miles.	Buffalo. Miles.
		l. 7 miles, *Cayuga Bridge*. and the Steam-Boat on Cayuga Lake. There is a regular Stage, twice a day, from Montezuma to the Bridge, fare 50 cents; and thence to *Geneva, Canandaigua*, &c. fare 4 cents a mile. See *Cayuga Lake*.		
205	97	l. mouth of Clyde R., or Canandaigua Outlet, [close on the left to Clyde V.,] .	63	157
210	102	Lock No. 63, rise 9 feet, W. extremity of Seneca R. Level, Galen, .	58	152
215	107	*Clyde V.*, 'Old Block House,' on Clyde R., Lock No. 64, rise 5 feet, Town of Galen, now Wayne Co., .	53	147
219½	111½	Lock No. 65, rise 7 feet, .	48½	142½
224	116	*Lyons V*, cap. Wayne Co., Lock No. 66, rise 6 feet, .	44	138
		l. Canandaigua Outlet.		
225¼	117¼	Lock No. 67, rise 10 feet, in Lyons, Lower Aqueduct ov. Mud Creek, .	42¾	136¾
229½	121½	3 Locks, Nos. 68, 69, 70, each 8, rise 24 feet in ¼ mile, .	37¾	132½
230¼	122¼	*Newark V.*, in T. of Lyons, formerly Phelps, .	37	131¾
239	131	l. *Palmyra V.*, Town of Palmyra, now Wayne Co., .	29	123
		l. 13 miles, *Canandaigua*, cap. Ontario County. There is a regular daily Stage, connected with the Packet Boats, fare 75 cents; and also to the *Sulphur Springs*, fare not known.		
240¼	132¼	Upper Aqueduct over Mud Creek, Macedon, .	27¾	121¾
242¾	134¾	Lock No. 71, rise 10 feet, .	25¼	119¼

Albany. Miles.	Utica. Miles.		Rochester. Miles.	Buffalo. Miles.
243½	135½	Lock No. 72, rise 10 feet, Macedon, Wayne County, .	24½	118½
252	144	Fullam's Basin, Perrinton, Monroe County, . .	16	110
254	146	Hartwell's Basin, Perrinton,	14	108
256	148	*Great Embankment*, 72 feet, whole length near 2 miles, ov. Teoronto, or Irondequot Creek, Perrinton and Pittsford, ...	12	106
256½	148½	Lock No. 73, rise 8 feet, in Pittsford, . . .	11½	105½
258	150	*Pittsford Village*, Monroe Co.,	10	104
264½	156½	*Brighton Village*, Brighton, .	3½	97½
		Here are 5 Locks, in 1¼ mile, Nos 74, 75, 76, 77, 78, each 7.4 feet, rise 37 feet, 3½ to 2 miles from Rochester.		
		☞ At Lock No. 78, the *Genesee Level* of the Canal, 65 miles, commences, extending westward to Lockport, Niagara Co.		
267½	159½	l. Feeder from Genesee R., 2 m. in length, Brighton,	½	94½
		The River is navigable, above Rochester, 70 to 90 miles.		
267¾	159¾	*E. Rochester*, (now incorporated with Rochester V.,)	¼	94¼
		Aqueduct, over Genesee R. & Mill Canals, all of hewn stone, supported by eleven arches, rather the grandest single feature of the Canal.		
			Lockport. Miles.	
268	160	*Rochester*, cap. Monroe Co., T. of Gates, pop. in 1823, 3700, . . .	63	94
		r. Falls of Genesee R., well worth seeing, as are the Mills and Factories.		

Albany. Miles.	Rochester. Miles.		Lockport. Miles.	Buffalo. Miles.
		r. 7 m., Port Genesee, Lake Ontario Steam-Boat, which see.		
		There are Stages, in all directions, from this place, fare about 4 cents a mile.		
		For the best line in the State, of the same extent, on rather the best road, see *Ridge Road*, extending to Lewiston, 80 miles, fare $3 20. The road to Avon is also very good, and by Caledonia and Batavia to Buffalo, where there is also an excellent line of Stages. If going to Niagara Falls, and intending to go by land, from Rochester, I would take the Ridge Road line westward to Lewiston, and approach the Falls from below, as the view is more interesting. *See page 52.*		
		☞ The distances, from Brockport to Buffalo, have not yet been measured, on the Towpath, and may vary some from those here given, obtained from the Engineers. When I was along this line, in July, 1824, taking notes for this little Pocket convenience, it was supposed the water would be let in, to Lockport, by Sept. 1, 1824.		
274½	6½	King's Basin, Greece, r. 1½ mile, Eldredge's, Ridge Road.	56½	87½
277	9	Webber's Basin, Ogden,	54	85
278½	10½	Kilborn's Basin, Ogden, [2 m. from Ridge Road,] .	52½	83½
280	12	Spencer's Basin, Ogden, .	51	82

Albany. Miles.	Rochester. Miles.		Lockport. Miles.	Buffalo. Miles.
		r. 1¾ mile, Parma V., Ridge Road.		
281	13	Webster's Basin, Ogden, .	50	81
283	15	Bates V., Sweden, Embankment Salmon Creek, .	48	79
		r. 2¼ miles, Ridge Road.		
285½	17½	Cooley's Basin, Sweden, .	45½	76½
		r. 1½ mile, Ridge Road.		
287¾	19¾	*Brockway*, or Brockport, Sweden, Monroe County, .	43¼	74¼
		The navigation of the Canal terminated here, from the autumn of 1823, to that of 1824.		
		r. 1½ m., ClarksonV., on Ridge Road.		
		l. 17 miles, Le Roy V., on old Stage Road, from Buffalo eastward.		
		☞ Why not Brockway, the name of the man from whom it is named, and not Brockport? When the Canal is completed, this place will be much more like a *way* than a *port*.		
293¼	25¼	*Holley V.*, Murray, Genesee County; *High Embankment*, 73 feet, over Sandy Creek,	37¾	68¾
		r. 3 miles, Ridge Road.		
299½	31½	Smith's Basin, Murray, on transit line, [*Halfway Basin*,] .	31½	62½
302½	34½	Sandy Creek Embankment, Gaines, . . .	28½	59½
303½	35½	*Newport V.*, Gaines, . .	27½	58½
		r. 2½ m., Gaines V., on Ridge Road.		
304½	36½	Gaines Basin, . .	26½	57½
305½	37½	Otter Creek Embankment, 55 feet, . , .	25½	56½

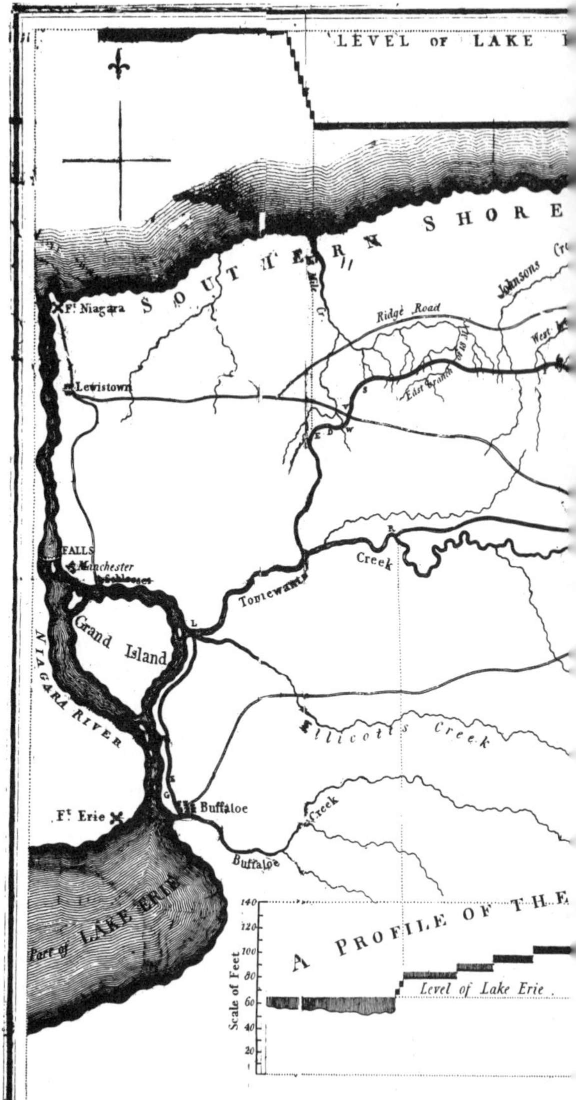

LEVEL OF LAKE

SOUTHERN SHORE

Johnsons Cre

Ft Niagara

Ridge Road

West

Lewistown

East Branch

FALLS

Manchester

Schlosser

Creek

Tonewanta

Grand Island

NIAGARA RIVER

Ellicott's Creek

Ft Erie

Buffaloe

Creek

Buffaloe

Part of LAKE ERIE

A PROFILE OF THE

Level of Lake Erie.

Scale of Feet

140
120
100
80
60
40
20

Kensett Sculp

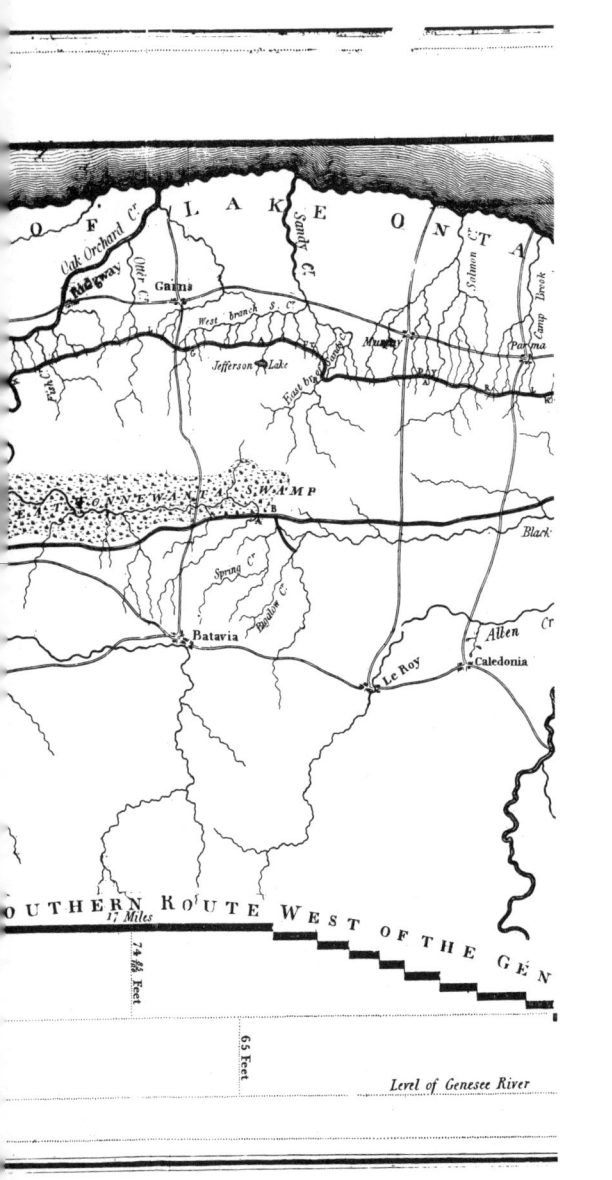

OF LAKE ONTA

Oak Orchard Cr
Ridgway
Gaines
Otter Cr
West branch S. Cr
Sandy Cr
Salmon Cr
Camp
Parma
Jefferson Lake
East branch
Murray
Payn

TONEWANTA SWAMP
B
A
Black

Spring Cr
Bigtline Cr

Batavia
Allen
Cr
Le Roy
Caledonia

SOUTHERN ROUTE WEST OF THE GEN
17 Miles

74½ Feet

65 Feet

Level of Genesee River

Albany. Miles.	Rochester. Miles.		Lockport. Miles.	Buffalo. Miles.
307	39	Clarke's Brook, long Embankment, 15 feet, Gaines,	24	55
310	42	*Arch Road-way*, under Canal, [the only one,] and Fish Creek Embankment, Ridgeway, . . .	21	52
		r. 2½ miles, Oak Orchard V., Ridge Road.		
312	44	Aqueduct over Oak Orchard Creek, and Feeder, half a mile in length, Ridgeway, . . .	19	50
		l. 5½ m., Shelby, New Channel for Tonnewanta Creek, Feeder, 100 feet in width, 4½ m., from Tonnewanta V. through T. Swamp.		
		r. Falls Oak Orchard Creek; and 3½ miles, Ridgeway V., Ridge Road.		
314½	46½	Servoss's Basin & Inn, Ridgeway, Genesee County, .	16½	47½
		¼ m. Embankment ov. Middle Branch, Oak Orch. Creek.		
317¾	49¾	Middleport, [another port,] Royalton, Niagara County,	13¼	44¼
		¼ mile, Embankment over W. Branch Oak Orch. Creek.		
319½	51½	Johnson's Creek Embankment, 25 feet, .	11½	42½
322½	54½	Embankment over 18 Mile Creek, 20 feet, Royalton, .	8½	39½
323½	55½	——— Basin, Royalton	7½	38½
331	63	*Lockport*, cap. Niagara Co., pop. in 1823, 1458; W. end 65 Mile Level, Ravine Basin, 6 acres, 30 feet,		31

The Canal here ascends the *Mountain Ridge*, from the Genesee Level to that of Lake Erie, the latter 31 m., by 5 double combined Locks, each 12.4 feet rise, Nos. 79, 80, 81, 82, 83,

rise 62 feet.* The Ravine, through
which the Canal rises the Mountain
Ridge, is a singular and interesting
curiosity.

Here is the *Back Bone* of the Erie
Canal, which will hardly be completed, I am afraid, by the close of
1825. Some part of it may, and I
give its distances, as nearly exact as
they can be known, before being
measured on the Tow-path.

☞ There are no good roads leading
from Lockport; but there will be
by-and-by; and daily Stages, by the
summer of 1825. When will the
road, on the Mountain Ridge to the
Falls, be finished?

☞ When at Lockport, in July, I was
told the Canal would be navigated,
from Brockport to this place, early
in September, and that there would
then be a daily Stage to and from
Buffalo.

1. 2½ m., Cold Spring, on the old ' Indian Path,' and the brow of the
Mountain Ridge,—a lodging-place
for travellers, in 1797, when there
were no houses W. of Genesee R.

Albany	Lockport		Buffalo
333	2	Deepest Cutting on Mount. Ridge, 31 feet 4 inches, averaging about 26 feet, for near 3 miles of rock: geodiferous limerock, . .	29
336	5	two Sulphur Springs, Niagara, .	26
338	7	r. *Pendleton V.*, Niagara, . .	24

Here the Canal enters the Tonnewanta
Creek, which it follows 12 miles, to
the Dam, the Creek having had but
1 foot descent, in this distance. Tow-
path on the left, or S. side. This C.
is the boundary of Niagara and Erie
Counties, and of the Towns of Niagara, Amherst, and Buffalo.

* Originally laid out 60 feet,

Albany. Miles.	Lockport. Miles.		Buffalo. Miles.
350	19	Dam, 4 feet 6 inches, just below the mouth of Ellicott's Creek, Locks to enter Niagara River, at Milltown,	12
		r. Tonnewanta, and Grand Island, Niagara River.	
352½	21½	lower end Long Meadows, 4½ m., at 2 Mile Creek, Buffalo, Erie County,	9½
358½	27½	r. lower end proposed *Black Rock Harbor, Sloop Lock*, Conjocketa Creek,	3½
		r. Squaw Island, and Mole, W. side Basin.	
359½	28½	*Black Rock V.*, Buffalo, and Ferry over Niagara River, half a mile,	2½
		r. over R., Waterloo V., of Upper Canada.	
360½	29½	r. *Bird Island*, in Niagara River, upper end of the Mole for forming Black Rock Harbor, or the Buffalo Harbor, as it will be called by-and-by, if it make a harbor,	1½
362	31	Buffalo, cap. Erie County, Buffalo Creek, Light House, Lake Erie, Mole, Upper Harbor; pop. 1300.	

r. over the Lake, *Fort Erie*, of Upper Canada.

There are 2 lines of daily Stages to the Falls of Niagara and Lewiston, noticed under *Ridge Road:* and there are Stages, from Buffalo, in all directions,—fare, generally, 4 cents a mile. In September, there will be a daily Stage to and from Lockport, to the close of navigation this season.

☞ The times of arrival and departure of the Steam-Boat on Lake Erie, not exactly known, nor the prices of passage.

And here, after a long journey, *all the way* from New-York to Buffalo, 507 miles,—145 by the Steam-Boat, the *very shortest distance*, and *almost* 362 by the Canal, (for it is not yet *quite finished*) by the Canal Packet,—here let us pause a little, and rest, while we look about us, and indulge in some reflections. Steam-navigation, and Canals, are working mighty changes in the aspect of things and in business. We see this every where; but here, and on these extended lines of commerce, more than any where else. Let us turn over a few pages of the Book of Fate, and read what Mother Nature long since decreed.

All hail to thee, New-York, thou Queen of Cities of the New World ! What Nature had indicated, for the extension of thy sphere of power, and its perpetuity, but left undone, Art has almost effected, and soon will perfectly accomplish. This done, there will arise, far in the West, a twin-sister of thine, and yet not thy rival, though almost thy equal, in power, numbers, and splendor. Hail to thee, Buffalo, unrivalled sister, Queen of the Cities of the West ! In thy very infancy, thou hast drunk deep of the cup of affliction, and hast felt the rod of chastisement and the hand of the oppressor : but fear not ;—thy destiny is fixed, thy high destiny,—second, only, in rank, in numbers, power, riches, and magnificence, to thy elder sister of the Isles of the Sea.

But,—let us return to New-York, and retrace this long line. There was a time,—but that was when the Republic was young, or yet unborn, or, ' puking and mewling in the nurse's arms,' when the head of Sloop-navigation, on the Hudson, was fixed upon, in the minds of many, as the extreme limit of the commerce of the metropolis. Here, then, arose Cities, fair to the eye, confident in the felicity of local position, and in the enjoyment of advantages, commanding, and that were to last for ever. Genius, however, and science, called Steam-Boats into existence, and experience soon whispered the inhabitants of those cities to be rather less confident and presuming. Under the dominion of genius and science, which regards the prosperity and the happiness of the many, as of more importance than that of the few,—of the whole, as greater than any part,—the Canals have been called into existence, and are completing what Steam-navigation only began. What those Towns, on the Hudson, once were, to the western regions of this State, Buffalo will soon be, to the immense regions around the shores of the Lakes of the West, Erie, Huron, Michigan, Superior, and the vallies of the Missouri, and of the upper Mississippi. Here is the contrast, in extent, and the ground-work of comparative operation and prospective power. Let us turn over a few more pages, just dipping into probabilities, and conversing a little with the future, as with the past.

In passing up the Hudson, if my visual optics, dimmed somewhat by age, do not mislead my mental vision, I see something like a new Town, at the head of Ship-navigation;—but we must pass this, and go westward. What Schenectady has been, of late, to Albany, her old rival must now be to New-York, and make the most of it. What all those old Towns have been, to the Western Country, with Utica, and the trading Towns of the West, New-York is, now, excepting only in a limited degree. Transhipments, to be sure, make some business; but agencies, and commissions, and factorage, do not replace, in amount of profits, that which has been lost by changes in the mode of business. If any thing were yet wanting to ensure these results, Monopoly will supply all the rest, in grasping at every thing.

At Syracuse, if I am not again misled, a vast space is covered with buildings, as if here were to be a great City, embracing Salina, and Geddesburgh, and Liverpool in a sort of suburb. At Rochester, also, I pause a little, to look at its mills and factories, its shops, offices, and steeples, embracing much business and a great population, but less wide-spread than the City of Salt. Thence passing to Buffalo, excepting only Lockport, all these new *ports* seem only old *ways;*—and so here we are, once more, at this Port of the American Mediterranea, fully impressed with the persuasion, that the effect of Steam-navigation, and Canals, will be to make two great commercial Cities, and two only. Excepting at those two points, there are no very commanding positions, or none that will operate, to any great extent around them, so as to give exclusive advantages for commerce; and as to mere trade, every part enjoys its benefits so equally, as to leave, either no preference, or, so many, as to amount to none.

A passing word to the changes we have witnessed. But a few years since, this whole region was a wilderness:—not a house, in 1797, from Genesee River to this place, and here only a few huts for Indian traders. I *almost* remember the time, when the German Flats, which we passed

E

on the Mohawk, and *perfectly*, when Whitesborough was considered the very end, the extreme limit of ' the Westward,'—then Onondaga, Geneva, Canandaigua, the Genesee River, and finally Buffalo, into which the stream of emigration has long been pouring its almost countless numbers, and yet that stream is not exhausted, nor is ' the Westward' half full of people. The country around this place is not yet half stocked with inhabitants: Erie County has but 17 to a square mile. And yet I see that the stream of emigration rolls on, farther West, and would inquire, Where, now, is the end of ' the Westward ?' Here are passing, as I should suppose, 500 persons, each day, all going *west*, and that in July, a season of the year rather early for the pouring out of the full stream. From all I have observed, there must be about 1000 strangers, constantly in this village, just arrived, all in a bustle. But what will be the bustle, here, some 50 or 100 years hence, when the countries, all around these Lakes, shall contain 17 to 50 persons per square mile !

RIDGE ROAD.

THE line of Mail Stages, on this road, between *Lewiston* and *Rochester*, is one of the best in the State, as the road also is; fare, 4 cents a mile. This line is a part of one that runs from Lewiston to Albany, and back, each way in 4 days, as below. Leaves Lewiston every day, at 3 A. M., and reaches Rochester same day, at 8 P. M.; leaves Rochester at 3 A. M., and reaches Auburn at 8 P. M.; leaves Auburn at 3 A. M., and reaches Utica at 8 P. M.; leaves Utica at 3 A. M., and reaches Albany at 8 P. M. of the 4th day. Returning, in the same order and time.

	Miles.	Total.
Lewiston to Cambria,	15	
Hartland, (7 miles from Lockport,)	11	26
Oak Orchard,	14	40
Gaines,	7	47
Sandy Creek,	8	55
Clarkson,	7	62
Parma,	7	69
Greece,	6	75
Rochester, (1st day, on Ridge Road,)	5	80
Pittsford,	8	88
Mendon,	7	95
Canandaigua,	15	110
Geneva,	16	126
Cayuga Bridge,	14	140
Auburn, (2d day,)	9	149
Skaneateles,	7	156
Onondaga,	17	173
Manlius,	10	183
Vernon,	24	207
Utica, (3d day,)	15	222
Albany, (4th day,)	96	318

Between *Lewiston* and *Buffalo* there are regular Stages, twice each day; fare the same, on either side of the river; but passengers pay their own ferriage, if they cross the river. To see the Falls, to the best advantage, go from Lewiston to Whitney's; and after going on to the Islands, cross the river immediately below the Falls, ferriage 25 cents, descending and ascending the stairways. In my opinion, the best *single view* is from Forsyth's piazza, on the Canada side.

From Lewiston to Niagara Falls, 7 miles, passing the Devil's Hole; Tonnewanta Creek, and the Erie Canal, 11; Black Rock, 10; Buffalo, $2\frac{1}{2}$; $=30\frac{1}{2}$.

Lewiston to Queenston, 1 m., ferriage 18 cents; Forsyth's, at the Falls, passing the Queenston Heights, Brock's Monument, the Battle Ground, and Whirlpool, 7; thence by a very pleasant road, by Chippewa, to Waterloo, 18; ferry to Black Rock, 18 cents; Buffalo, $2\frac{1}{2}$, $=28\frac{1}{2}$ miles.

CHAMPLAIN CANAL.

———

Juncta, junction of the Champlain with the Erie Canal, 8½ miles from Albany, 2½ from Troy, - See *Juncta,* under *Erie Canal.*   63½

l. Erie Canal, at the 'Nine Locks,' 2 below, and 7 above the junction.

½   r. Whiting's Mill, and the Cotton Factory; [l. ½ mile, Cahoos Bridge, and Falls, 1 mile,] -   63

Dam, Mohawk River, 7 feet, Pond 1600 feet wide, back water 53 rods: Navigation through this Pond; Guard Locks, Feeder for Erie Canal, - - -   63

2   l. G. Van Schoonhoven, and Wind Mill, W. side V. of Waterford,   61½

r. *Waterford V.,* Demarest's, and Bridge over HUDSON RIVER, which see.

r. Side-Cut to Mohawk River, 3 Locks, in Waterford, descent 32.7 feet; distance to the Sloop Lock, upper end of Troy, 3 miles, for which see HUDSON RIVER.

Stages run, in summer, daily, from Waterford to the Springs of Saratoga County; to Ballston Spa, 21½ ; to Saratoga Springs, 24 miles.

e 2

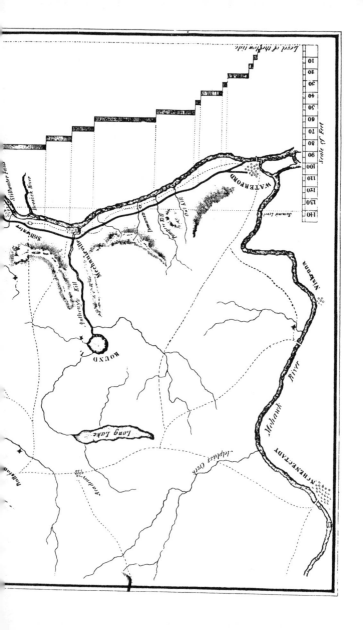

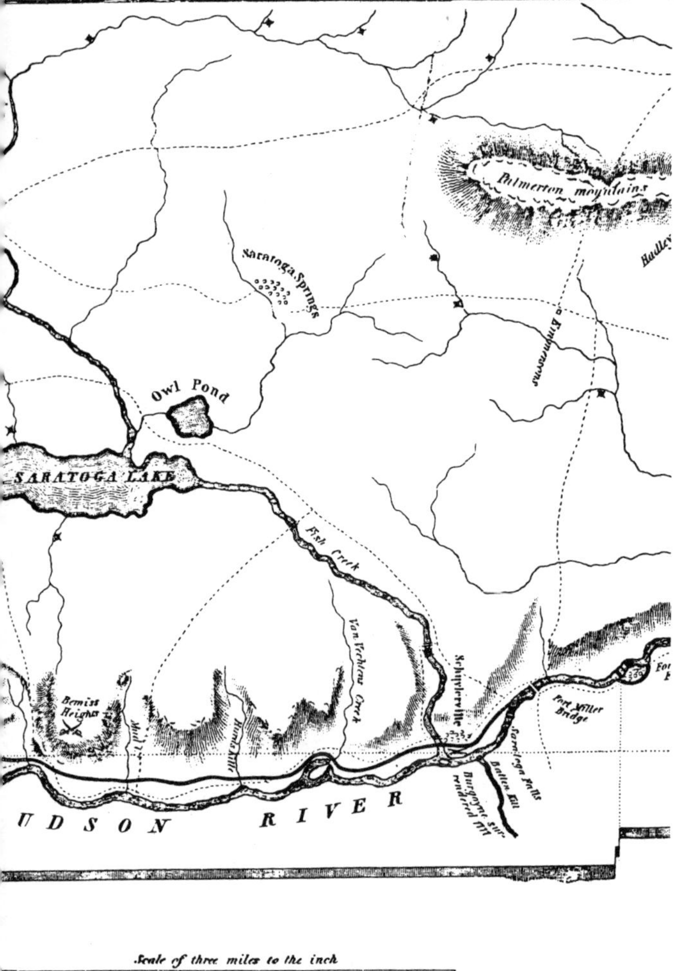

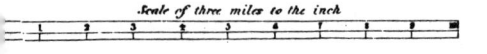

Palmerton mountains

Bailley

Saratoga Springs

Owl Pond

SARATOGA LAKE

Fish Creek

Van Vechten Creek

Schuylerville

Bemist Heights

Fort Miller Bridge

Saratoga Falls

Batten Kill

Burgoyne's 2d
entrenched off

HUDSON RIVER

Scale of three miles to the inch

| 1 | 2 | 3 | 4 | 5 | 6 | 7 | 8 | 9 | 10 |

Copy-right secured

3¼	The ' Three Locks,' Waterford, Nos. 1, 2, 3, rise 26½ feet, -	59¾
5½	Culvert, Peebles' Farm, -	58
6¼	Lock No. 4, rise 9 feet, Halfmoon, Culvert, - - - -	57¼
10¼	r. *Borough*, Vernam's, Halfmoon,	53¼
10½	r. *Mechanicville*, Stillwater, Culvert, Anthony's Kill, - -	53
	r. Cotton Factory.	
	r. Cross's, Stage House.	
10¾	l. Creek Road, by Dunning Street to the Springs; 12½ miles to Ballston Spa, and 15¼ to Saratoga Springs.	
12	Lock No. 6, rise 9 feet, Stillwater,	51½
12¾	r. ov. River, mouth Hoosac River, Schaghticoke, - - -	50¾
13½	*Stillwater Village*, Waste Wear, -	50
	r. Wing Dams, and Mills on Hudson River; Stillwater Falls.	
16	l. Bemus's Heights, battle ground, Oct. 7, 1777, Willard Farm, -	47½
18	l. ¾ mile, battle ground, Sept. 19, 1777, Freeman Farm, - -	45½
	Morris, or Fly Farm, fenced, *in the air*, with rows of the poplar.	
19	r. Smith's, the house in which Gen. Fraser died in 1777, [formerly a farm-house, near the battle ground, the 'Swords house,' in 'Burgoyne's Expedition,' owned by the father of the Messrs. Swords. New York,] - -	44½
	l. on the hill, Gen. Fraser's grave.	
23	l. Van Deusen's, Saratoga, - -	40½

　　l. Road to Saratoga Springs, good,
　　　　11 miles, by Stafford's Bridge,
　　　　7 miles.

26　　Seat of the late Gen. Schuyler,　-　37½
　　　Schuylerville, Fish Creek Aqueduct,
　　　　Mills, Eastman and Houghton's
　　　　Rotary Saw-mill.

　　l. 11 miles to Saratoga Springs, 18
　　　　to Ballston Spa.

26½　r. Fort Hardy, scene of Burgoyne's
　　　　surrender, Oct. 17, 1777; l. the
　　　　Burgoyne Basin, or the *Gates
　　　　Basin*, ' as you please,' -　　-　37

　　It should be observed, in passing, that
　　　　the military works of that day,
　　　　walls of earth, thrown up in haste,
　　　　are found on nearly all the sum-
　　　　mits of the River Hill, from a little
　　　　below Bemus's Heights, to Fort
　　　　Miller, and some above, princi-
　　　　pally, however, thence northward,
　　　　on the east side of the Hudson.
　　　　Many of them may be seen from
　　　　the Canal, and the Stage road, a
　　　　very pleasant one, close along
　　　　side.

27　　l. ov. R., mouth Battenkill,　-　-　36½
28　　Northumberland Collector's Office,
　　　　' Guard Gates,' Dam, head Sa-
　　　　ratoga Falls, where the Canal
　　　　enters the River by 2 Guard
　　　　Locks, at Vanderzee's Store;
　　　　fine Pike Fishery, -　　-　-　35½

　　r. Cramer and Granger's Mills.

　　l. to Saratoga Springs 12, Ballston
　　　　Spa 18 miles.

The Navigation here takes the River, 3
 miles, to Fort Miller, on the E.
 side, where there is a Dam, at
 Fort Miller Falls, a Canal of about
 half a mile, 2 Locks, Nos. 7 & 8,
 rise 18 feet, and Guard Locks;
 thence again it takes the River,
 8 miles, to the Village of Fort
 Edward.

A Horse-Boat is employed in towing
 Boats on the River.

A Canal will probably soon be made,
 on the E. side, from the Guard
 Locks, head of Saratoga Falls, to
 Fort Edward, 11 miles, having
 either a Bridge Tow-path, a Rope-
 ferry, or an Aqueduct, over the
 River, at the head of these Falls.

28½	Fort Miller Bridge, - - -	35
31	Fort Miller Canal, ½ m., 2 Locks, and Guard Locks, in Town of Fort Edward, - - -	32½
34½	r. mouth Moses Kill, - - -	29
36	l. mouth Snook Kill, - - -	27½
39½	*Fort Edward Village*, 3 Locks, Nos. 9, 10, 11, rise 30 feet,	24

 l. *Fort Edward*, on bank of Hudson, built in 1755, by Gens. Ly-
 man and Johnson, at the Old
 'Landing,' or 'CarryingPlace,'
 of the French Wars.

Just above this is the *Great Dam*,
 27 feet high, 900 feet in length,
 across the Hudson, for supplying the summit level of this
 Canal with water. It cost

about $ 30,000. E. end, Me-
lanchton Wheeler's Mills.

There is now a *Packet Boat*, the Superior, on the Canal between Fort
Edward and Whitehall, running
in connexion with the Steam-Boat
on Lake Champlain, which see.
It is connected, also, with the Albany and Whitehall Coach Line,
Office 365 N. Market-street, Albany. Stages leave Albany every
Monday and Friday morning,
meet the Packet at Fort Edward,
which reaches Whitehall on the
same days, at evening, through in
one day. The Packet leaves
Whitehall every Tuesday and Saturday morning, on the arrival of
the Steam Boat, proceeds to Fort
Edward, where Stages are adver-
tised to be in waiting for Albany,
Saratoga and Ballston Springs.
Fort Edward to Sandy Hill, 2
miles, thence to Saratoga Springs,
20; regular Stages, in summer,
from Baird's,—fare $ 1 25.

40   1. Feeder, from above the Great
Dam, ½ m. in length, -   -   23½
1. Road to Sandy Hill, Glen's Falls,
and Lake George.
Pine Tree, where Miss M‘Crea
was killed, in the Revolution-
ary War.

42   1. proposed Navigable Feeder, 7
miles in length, from the Hudson R. above Glen's Falls, not
yet finished; see Queensbury,

Jessups Landing

Fort George

Falls

Halfway Brook

Glens Falls

Bakers Falls

Snook Kill

Stone for Locks

Sandy Hill

Kingsbury

Kingsbury

Black Town

Moses Kill

Crockers

t Miller alls

The Kingsbury

Canal

Swamp

𝕸𝖆𝖕 and 𝕻𝖗𝖔𝖋

of the Champlain canal as MADE

TO THE HUDSON

and SURVEYED thence to the tide

Ja. Geddes Engine

1820

Rawdon sc. NY

LAKE GEORGE

LAKE

Iron works

Welch Hollow

South Bay

Fort Ann

Uninhabited tract of Rocky mountains

Wood

Winchel

Creek

White Hall

Lake Level

rom Lake Champlain

IVER

t Waterford By

RR Feet 10 inches

in the Gazetteer; [1. Sandy Hill V. 1½ m., Glen's Falls, 4½.] - - - - -   21½

42½   Fort Edward Creek, and Kingsbury Swamp, [8 miles,] -   21

47½   r. Wood Creek, and along the right, to Fort Anne, - - -   16½

     l. 2½ m. Kingsbury V., 2 miles N. of which is Putnam Field.

51½   l. *Fort Anne V.*, 3 Locks, Nos. 12, 13, 14, fall 24 feet, into Wood Creek, - - - -   12

     l. mouth of Half-Way Brook, and 7 miles, Lake George Mountains.

The Wood Creek Navigation, 3½ m., and a Lock of 4 feet descent, thence again in Wood Creek, 3 miles, to the Canal of 5½ miles, along the W. side of Wood Creek, to Whitehall V. and Landing, 12 miles from Fort Anne.

55   Lock No. 15, fall 4 feet, *Dam Lock*, Narrows, Wood Creek.   8½

58   Dam, in Wood Creek, to supply the Canal to Whitehall, and make the Creek navigable, 3 miles above, to the Dam-Lock,   5½

62   r. E. side Wood Creek, mouth Pawlet River, from Vermont,   1½

63½   *Whitehall Village*, head of Lake Champlain, 3 Locks, Nos. 16, 17, 18, fall 26 feet to the Lake.

     2 m., l., South Bay, and the trophies of M'Donough's Victory.

For distances, &c., northward from here, see Lake Champlain Steam-Boat; New-York to Albany, 145½ miles; Albany to Juncta, by Erie Canal, 8½ = 154; thence to Whitehall, 63½ = 217½ miles from New-York to Whitehall.

There are regular lines of Sloops, on Lake Champlain, one or more of which is said to be always in waiting for freight and passengers. The Steam-Boat, with its trips, fare, &c., is noticed under *Lake Champlain Steam-Boat;* and the Canal Packet, Superior, at *Fort Edward,* under CHAMPLAIN CANAL, with the Stages, &c., to Albany and the Springs.

☞ The Steam-Boat *Mountaineer,* on *Lake George,* is built on *Annesley's* plan.

INDEX.

F

f 2

ERRATA.

Page 13, for Coeyman's, *read* Coeymans.
   29, ,, Cohoos Falls, ,, Cahoos Falls,.
   32, ,, Root's,   ,, Roof's.
   34, ,, Gniess,   ,, Gneiss.

☞ A WORD TO TOURISTS.—Strangers visiting the City of New York, and intending to make the ' *Grand Tour*,' or to travel through any part of this State, would do well to repair to GOODRICH'S *Geographical and Map Establishment*, 124 Broadway, where they can, at once, supply themselves with maps, geographical and topographical publications, itineraries, &c.

The best large Map of this State, is *Eddy's*, improved by Goodrich, to the present time. I have seen a very good *Map of the Northern States and the Canadas*, now in the hands of the engraver, by Goodrich, which will be published shortly: it extends S. to include Pennsylvania, embraces all the States to the N. and E., and on the N. extends to Quebec. *Vance's Map*, of the western part of New-York, is also a good one. *Akerly's Geology of the Hudson River*, and *Goodrich's Map*, in book; and Hooker's neat little Map of the City, done up in morocco, for the pocket, should at least be brought to the notice of strangers, as accurate and useful companions; as should *Randel's Map*, of the Island of New-York, the Bay, Harbor, &c.

I suppose I may now name my own publications, the *Gazetteer and Geography of the State of New York*, noticed in the Preface, and this *Pocket Guide*, on both which I have bestowed time, and money, and labor enough, to have made them, with competent talents, instructive and interesting companions.

———

☞ TO MY PATRONS.—While travelling, to collect materials for my Pocket Guide, through the Canals, the Hudson River, &c., I experienced every kindness and attention from the Captains of

Canal Packets, and Steam-Boats, the Proprietors, and many others, to whom my best acknowledgments are due. I shall send copies of this work to many of them, with this general request for their assistance. They will please have the goodness to note any errors they may discover, or omissions, and to send me their notices, at Troy. The Proprietors of Steam-Boats, Packets, and Stages, *throughout the State*, would confer a favor by giving me early notice of the arrangements of their several lines.